John W. Truesdell

Bottom Facts Concerning The Science Of Spiritualism

John W. Truesdell

Bottom Facts Concerning The Science Of Spiritualism

ISBN/EAN: 9783742858931

Manufactured in Europe, USA, Canada, Australia, Japa

Cover: Foto ©ninafisch / pixelio.de

Manufactured and distributed by brebook publishing software (www.brebook.com)

John W. Truesdell

Bottom Facts Concerning The Science Of Spiritualism

CONTENTS.

CHAPTER I.
"IF A MAN DIE SHALL HE LIVE AGAIN?"
Evidences of immortality............................. 17

CHAPTER II.
TO THE INVESTIGATOR.
What is a spiritual medium? Where mediums are to be found.. 23

CHAPTER III.
LAWS OF THE SPIRIT CIRCLE.
Conditions to be observed. How to communicate with spirits. The A B C of investigation. Necessity of mature media........... 25

CHAPTER IV.
OBSTACLES TO BE ENCOUNTERED.
The author's first experience in investigation.—Apparent evidence of fraud.—Too hasty conclusions.—A lost opportunity.—How a spirit moves ponderable substances.—Allen Kardec.—How spirits make mistakes.—Involuntary muscular action............... 36

CHAPTER V.
PERISPRIT.
Its utility at materializations.—An indispensable factor in all circles. —Latest information.—How it is generated.—Its potency.—Its penetrability.—Loss of energy in its generation.—New discovery. —How it may be stored up for future use.—Unit of its measurement.—Its power of attenuation.—Its uses 43

CONTENTS

CHAPTER VI.
THE DIAKKA.

A sketch of his character, by the spirit of James Victor Wilson.—Various opinions as to his origin.—An ancient record 51

CHAPTER VII.
THE HOME OF THE DIAKKA

"The Great Draco Major Belt."—Its beauties and magnitude, by Andrew Jackson Davis.—A later, and more accurate account, by the author's spirit-guide "Muhlenburg." 60

CHAPTER VIII.
MARY ANDREWS, THE MORAVIA MEDIUM.

A report of her seances published in the year 1871, by the author.—Ignorance of the investigator.—Mistaken evidences of fraud.—The works of the Diakka.—An apology.—Spirit lights.—Irresponsibility of mediums.—A spirit voice mistaken for that of the medium.—An unprejudiced report, by T. R. Hazard.—Extraordinary speech by the spirit of Daniel Webster.—Skepticism of the Diakka 63

CHAPTER IX.
REDEEMING QUALITIES OF THE DIAKKA.

His employment by higher spirits.—His devotion to mediums.—He personates Confucius.—He works for the "good of the cause."—An important meeting held by a band of Diakka.—Rapid transit.—The materialized suit of clothes.—A sensitive medium.—Materialization of a bank-note.—Insurmountable obstacles.—An opportune moment.—Dematerializing extraordinary 93

CHAPTER X.
SCIENCE VERSUS SPIRITUALISM.

Mistaken opinions.—Spiritualism courts investigation.—Scientists anxious to know the "Bottom Facts." 109

CHAPTER XI.
THE GREAT MATERIALIZED STONE.

An important inquiry.—Speech by Muhlenburg.—"Dead control."—The medium paralyzed by Muhlenburg's Perisprit.—World-

making.—Materializing extraordinary.—Another account, or
"*Bottom Facts*," by a Diakka.................................. 116

CHAPTER XII.
SEANCES WITH CHARLES H. FOSTER.
First interview.—The ballot-test.—Astounding revelations.—The
spirits deceived.—Suspicious circumstances.—Second interview.—
Complications increase.— Third interview.—The pellet-test.—
Medium trapped by the Diakka.—A storm of words, followed by a
calm.—A new discovery.—Reflections........................ 133

CHAPTER XIII.
INTERVIEWS WITH DR. HENRY SLADE.
Startling manifestations.—Slate-writing.—Fears of the doctor.—
A spirit hand.—A spirit message.—Suspicion of a Diakka.—A
dissatisfied investigator.—A second interview.—A decoy letter.—
Remarkable discovery.—Wonderful message from the spirit
world.—A trap.—The Diakka writes.—The spirits corrected.—
The victory.—A stormy session.—A calm.—The reconciliation.—
A remarkable disclosure.—The author ordained as a spiritual
medium... 143

CHAPTER XIV.
ONE OF THE AUTHOR'S MAIDEN SITTINGS.
A published report. — Slate-writing. — Ballot-test. — Raised letters
made to appear on the medium's arm.—A Diakka's explanation.. 160

CHAPTER XV.
A SEANCE WITH DELEGATES FROM THE ONEIDA COMMUNITY.
Startling results.—Spiritualists divided into two classes.—"The
world changing front."—A Diakka opinion.—Spirits getting "*en
rapport*" with the medium.—How the spirits write.—A challenge
to the world... 170

CHAPTER XVI.
LETTER FROM L. W. CHASE.
A wonderfully convincing seance.—The report corroborated.—An
explanation of the methods by a Diakka.—A beautiful experiment... 184

CHAPTER XVII

THE PARAFFINE-MOULD TEST.

A seance with Mrs. Mary Hardy.—The spirits beguiled.—A materialized hand (foot).—Paraffine seance by a Diakka............. 204

CHAPTER XVIII.

THE WONDERFUL EDDYS.

Exposures.—A stereotyped answer.—The curtain-test in the light circle.—Magnetized paraphernalia.—A remarkable exhibition.—Revelations by a Diakka.................................. 212

CHAPTER XIX.

ROPE-TYING TESTS.

Indian spirit-dance, by Olcutt.—The Diakka speaks.—The single and double-header spirit-knots................................. 228

CHAPTER XX.

THE COTTON-BANDAGE TEST.

Laura Ellis.—Annie Eva Fay.—The savants of Europe confounded.—A perfect hand-bill.—The "time-killer," or mellowing process.—Remarkable speech by a lady.—Seance extraordinary.—Power of the physical eye.—The man of many names.—The great front twist.—A smart skeptic.—True inwardness of the manifestations by a Diakka... 238

CHAPTER XXI.

SO-CALLED EXPOSURES.

Doctor Henry Slade.—His troubles in England.—Mistakes of the investigator.—An unfortunate letter.—Account from the Belleville, Ontario, Intelligencer.—A serious blow to the cause dealt by the Banner of Light.—Letter from a skeptic.—An error in judgment... 276

CHAPTER XXII.

TO SPIRITUAL MEDIUMS ONLY. ☞ CONFIDENTIAL.

The Author trusts to the honor of all readers,—except spiritual mediums,—that they will omit this chapter................. 308

TO THE READER.

THE following letters, which are a fair sample of many similar ones received by the author during the last few years, will serve as an introduction to the reader, and explain to him the purpose which accompanies the publication of this work.

The writer is among those who believe that everything in existence, from the lowest to the highest order, in the mineral, vegetable and animal kingdom, was created for a purpose; that nothing was ever made in vain, or ever can be; that of all known things created, Man is the most exalted, and that to his advancement, his power and his glory we should bend the most determined efforts of our lives.

The humblest person on this globe may be able to contribute something to the world's intelligence. If the author shall succeed in arresting the attention of a single reader for a period sufficient to save him from the fear of annihilation, or release him from the hell of any earthly superstition, the object of this book will have been fully accomplished.

LETTERS.

HARTFORD, CONN., January 11, 1882.

MR. JOHN W. TRUESDELL.

Dear Sir: Ten years ago, for the first time, I witnessed remarkable manifestations, commonly attributed to "spiritual forces," produced through your influence. A few weeks ago, I was again a close and interested observer of similar demonstrations; but, I am, to-day, as far from knowing their real cause, or your real views on this great subject, as ten years ago, when you first astonished and confounded my senses.

Desiring to again study the phenomena in your presence, I learn that you refuse to give any more sittings; and this, after your fame as an amateur has grown and strengthened for a period of twenty-five years—after your name has become authority in the best circles of all sections of the country.

How can you reconcile this position with your reputation as an earnest truth-seeker—as an investigator of the highest type? For, have you not uniformly refused to receive any money for your circles, giving freely of your time to many of our most prominent investigators, who have come from far and near to seek after the great truths supposed to underlie these manifestations? If you have decided to deprive the public of the opportunities you have, in the past, so freely extended to them, to study this great mystery under the best conditions, then you owe to them, and to yourself, the reasons for such decision, and the results of your experience, observation and study.

You have no moral right to withhold from your immense *clientele* the vast and valuable information you have gained during all these years.

Any statement coming from you would have incalculable value, as being that of a student, and not that of a professional medium who has used his gifts for money.

If you are convinced of the truth of the science, then it is your duty to give a waiting and earnest world the rules and methods that will insure exact and satisfying results to all who desire to enter into relations with the spirits of those who have "gone up higher." If, on the contrary, you have learned that all is vain, and that the portals of eternity are closed, save to those who enter the blessed realm, then far more do you owe to trusting, seeking, loving souls the knowledge that will lead them to await patiently the "lifting of the veil"—that will defend them from the cruel impositions of the unprincipled.

Yours for truth,

MARY J. GALT.

SALAMANCA, N. Y., October 10, 1882.

J. W. TRUESDELL.

Dear Friend: Since our interview at the Watkins Convention, I have been thinking of what you there said in relation to Spiritualism, and I am more than ever impressed with the idea that I then suggested—that you give the world the benefit of your investigations of that subject.

I know that you have spent years and much money in the investigation of Spiritualism. I am confident that you know as much about it as any other person in the country, and I think you owe it to the Cause of Truth, to give the public the benefit of your investigations. It matters not to me, whether your report shall prove a benefit to the spiritual cause, or a damage to it. What true Liberalism demands is the exact truth. You have the reputation among spiritualists, of being one of the very best of mediums, and among materialists, of being a first-rate necromancer. Yet all who know you personally have faith in your truthfulness as a man. Now, what I request is, that you give the general public, in some form, the benefit of your investigations.

If you would write a series of letters for some one of our Liberal journals, covering the whole subject, I can assure you they would be extensively read; or, if you should decide to put the knowledge you have acquired on this subject into book form, it would have a large sale.

Spiritualism, if it is a truth, is the grandest truth that was ever brought to the world. If it is a fraud, it is *the* fraud of the nineteenth century. Demonstrated immortality is what all people would like to witness. But every honest free-thinker will say, "*Let us have the truth at all hazards.*"

Truly yours,
H. L. GREEN.

SYRACUSE, July 20, 1882.

MR. JOHN W. TRUESDELL.

Dear Sir: The question as to the future existence of man is, at present, receiving much attention from all men of thinking minds, and a desire to obtain the results of your researches in the field of Spiritualism leads me to address you in behalf of "The Astro-Theological Society of the City of Syracuse," requesting that you will give us a statement of your views upon this question.

Having searched in vain for some proofs of man's immortality more trustworthy than that given by any system of religion or philosophy, we turn, as a last resort, to the consideration of the question as to the actual return of materialized spirit-forms, capable of proving their identity, as an intelligence existing apart from nature.

In view of the fact that you have devoted many years of your life to the study of this science—if it be a science—and that, during that time, you have never appeared before the public as a professional medium, or, in any manner, received pecuniary benefits from your investigations, any statements upon this subject, coming from you, will receive great consideration from the members of the Society which I have the honor to represent.

Hoping that you will favor us with a full expression of your views upon this question, either by a paper or an address, to be delivered at such time as shall be most convenient to yourself,

I am, yours truly,

J. D. MALLONEE,

President "Astro-Theological Society of the City of Syracuse."

LETTERS.

Boston, April 2, 1883.

John W. Truesdell, Esq.

Dear Sir: I learn that you are thinking of giving to the public, at last, the results of your twenty-five years of study, devoted to "Modern Spiritualism." I am heartily glad to learn this. I know of nothing in the modern world concerning which the people are in greater need of light.

It is either the grandest of revelations, or the most stupendous of frauds.

If it is true, the world ought to know it on the basis of indubitable proofs. If it be false, it is a base and heartless trifling with the most sacred memories and hopes; and those capable of knowingly helping it on ought to be treated as criminals and outcasts. He who is able to help the world to an intelligent decision of this important question will earn, and will deserve, the gratitude of thousands.

If you are this fortunate man, you are sincerely to be congratulated. Most truly,

Minot J. Savage.

BOTTOM FACTS

CONCERNING

THE SCIENCE OF SPIRITUALISM.

CHAPTER I.

"IF A MAN DIE, SHALL HE LIVE AGAIN?"

THIS has been, from time immemorial, among men, the question of all questions.

Religious teachers, representing every denomination in existence, have racked their brains, for centuries, in the vain effort to solve beyond a doubt this great problem, upon which is founded the structure of every religious creed. Philosophers in all ages have wrestled with the mystery, and men of science have spent their lives in vain attempts to accomplish its solution. They tell us that without the idea of future existence the present life is a miserable mockery, and that man, the grandest known achievement of the Creator, is a lamentable failure.

It is a sad compliment to humanity when we declare that our life is simply the result of a combination of materials, and that the death of the body is the end of all intelligent being!

Yet, when we instinctively ask for some positive assurance of life continued beyond the grave—something that will commend itself to our senses, proof more convincing than is furnished by cold, metaphysical reasoning, the philosopher looks wise and is silent.

Great men, who have spent their lives in endeavoring, by every art and device known to science, to unlock the hidden mysteries of the future, tell us that the very desire for life hereafter, which is the instinctive inheritance of every intelligent being, is among the best proofs of the theory which they have thus far discovered.

It is claimed that for every need known to the vegetable kingdom, and also for every necessity, emotion or hope known to the animal kingdom, there is, somewhere in this world, the possibility of its supply or gratification. Even a potato, lying in a dark cellar, demonstrates a need for light by sending out its long, tender sprouts in search of it, which fact, alone, proves that, somewhere, there is light ; and every plant which strikes its fibers down into the earth, or unfolds its leaves to the air, in search of moisture or nourishment, demonstrates, beyond question, that there exist in creation water and food to supply the demand.

So man, whose eye feels because there is light, whose ear hears because there is air to undulate, who hungers because there is food, who hates because there are ugly things in the world, and loves because there is so much that is loveable—asks for life beyond the grave, logically reasoning that we must be immortal, or that the desire for continued life would not be so eager and universal. Yet, when we appeal to these scientists for some proof beyond their cold philosophy, they too are dumb.

The priests, the so-called holy men of the church, who base their whole life-work upon the theory of man's immortality, have, for ages, claimed to know something of future life by means of the Word of God, which is said to have been made manifest thousands of years ago, through men divinely inspired. Yet, when some enthusiast ventures to suggest that to-day there are occurring in our very midst, phenomena more pointedly indicative of future life than any evidence to be found in old books or man-made creeds, these great moral teachers are among the first to doubt, if they fail to revile him.

Thus it will be seen that people of every religious opinion, and representing nearly every phase of society, believe in common the fact that the spirit lives after the death of the body, while they disagree only in their various methods of attempting to prove it. This want of harmony between the ultra orthodox Christian and the professed spiritualist seems to be more imaginary than real—founded more upon prejudice than fact. The breach is not near so wide as the opposing parties seem determined to make it appear. The Christian accepts, with scarcely a doubt, the inspired account of that ancient phenomenon the spirit hand-writing on the wall—mentioned in the book of Daniel—solely upon the evidence of one long-dead individual, while he smiles in derision at the millions of living witnesses who claim to have seen the same power made manifest by means of a common slate.

In turn, many of the spiritualists of to-day laugh to scorn those who are sufficiently credulous to accept as fact the miracles of the olden time, while they themselves do not hesitate to place implicit confidence in the so-called modern spiritual phenomena which are a hundred-fold more inexplicable.

It is not surprising that the frigid philosophy of the scientist, the profound metaphysical arguments of our great students, the simple quoting of divine authority, or the mere sophistry of many of our religious teachers, respecting the question of future life, is unsatisfactory to the masses—that the great army of truth-seekers (the middle class) yearn after some evidence more real and substantial.

CHAPTER II.

TO THE INVESTIGATOR.

NTICIPATING a few of the first questions which will naturally present themselves to the investigator, I answer:

First. A spiritual medium is a sensitive, impulsive person, usually of a social and affectionate nature, through whom, it is claimed, the spirits of our friends who have passed away may, in favorable circumstances, return and make themselves known to those yet in the material form.

Second. These mediums are more numerous than is generally supposed. Nearly every fairly-intelligent person is known to possess some latent mediumistic qualities, which, with proper attention and culture, would make him an approximate medium—though remarkable mediums, like true poets or great musicians, are by no means common.

To illustrate farther: let us measure perfection in musical talent by one hundred. A, is born into this world with ten talents and B. with twenty, while C. inherits ninety. Both A. and B., by close application, under favorable conditions, may so far improve upon their natural gifts as to be classed among the good musicians, but neither of them can ever hope to rank with a Mozart or a Beethoven.

Third. A spirit circle is formed by any number of individuals who may assemble for the purpose of developing media, or holding direct communication with those who have passed into spirit life.

CHAPTER III.

LAWS OF THE SPIRIT CIRCLE.

WHILE, as yet, we have been unable to discover and codify all the laws which must be observed to insure the occurrence of spirit phenomena, we are able to demonstrate beyond a shadow of doubt, by means of millions of experiments, running through years of experience, that certain conditions must be strictly observed in order that satisfactory phenomena may be manifested.

The following general rules, compiled from the writings of Emma Hardinge, James H. Young, and other spiritualists high in authority, will be interesting and instructive to the investigator, though they are not all strictly reliable, being subject to modification, from time to time, as we obtain new light from the spirit world:

"The first conditions to be observed relate to the persons who compose the circle. These should be, as far as possible, of opposite temperaments, as positive and negative in disposition, whether male or female; also of moral characters, pure minds, and not marked by repulsive points of either physical or mental condition. The physical temperaments should contrast with each other; but no person suffering from decidedly chronic disease, or of very debilitated *physique*, should be present at any circle, [Participate in any circle? AUTHOR.] unless it is formed expressly for healing purposes. I would recommend the number of the circle never to be less than three, nor more than twelve."*

The circle should be formed so as to balance as nearly as possible. When strangers are present whose dispositions are unknown to those in charge, they may be arranged at first, by way of experiment, according to their physical

---

* "Rules to be Observed when Forming Spiritual Circles," By Emma Hardinge.

or external appearance. For instance—a very fleshy and plethoric person, who is full of blood, should be seated next one who is spare and sallow, and a dark-haired, black-eyed individual next a blonde, irrespective of sex, although the latter distinction should not be entirely overlooked, as it is never desirable to seat more than three ladies side by side at any circle.

"The use growing out of the association of differing temperaments is to form a battery, on the principle of electricity or galvanism, composed of positive and negative elements. . . . . No person of a very strongly positive temperament or disposition should be present, as any such magnetic spheres emanating from the circle will overpower that of the spirits, who must always be positive to the circle in order to produce the phenomena. It is not desirable to have more than two already well-developed mediums in a circle, mediums always absorbing the magnetism of the rest of the party; hence, when there are too many present, the force, being divided, cannot operate successfully with any."

There is no great objection to the presence of any number of mediums, provided always they can unanimously agree upon one who shall act as conductor of the circle. Mediums, as a class, are prone to jealousy and fault-finding among themselves. Often, too, they are stubbornly skeptical in regard to every control except their own; and when several of them congregate at a single circle, unless they can agree upon a leader, and will consent to abide by his ruling, they will manage the circle with about the same success as would attend the movements of a vessel navigating unexplored waters under the guidance of half a score of captains.

"Never let the apartment be over-heated, or even close. As an unusual amount of magnetism is liberated at a circle, the room is always warmer than ordinary, and should be well ventilated. *Avoid strong light*, which, by producing excessive motion in the atmosphere, disturbs the manifestations. A very subdued light is the most favorable for manifestations of a magnetic character, especially for spiritual magnetism."

"If the circle is one which meets together periodically, and is composed of the same persons, let them always occupy the same seats (unless changed under spiritual direction), and sit (as the most favorable of all positions) round a table, their hands laid upon it, with palms downwards." (Except when the spirits are conversing with the medium by raps, when the hands should be shut, forming a fist, with the thumb folded inside, and pointing upwards.)

"It is believed that the wood, when charged, becomes a conductor, without the necessity of holding or touching hands. I should always suggest the propriety of employing a table as a conductor, especially as all tables in household use are more or less magnetically charged already.

"I recommend that the seance be opened

with music, vocal or instrumental, after which subdued, quiet and harmonizing conversation is better than wearisome silence : but let the conversation be always directed towards the purpose of the gathering, and never sink into discussion, or rise to emphasis—let it be gentle, quiet and spiritual, until phenomena begin to manifest."

"7. When motions of the table, or sounds, are produced freely, to avoid confusion, let one person only speak, and talk to the table as to an intelligent being. Let him, or her, tell the table that three tilts or raps mean 'Yes,' one means 'No,' and two mean 'Doubtful,' and ask whether the arrangement is understood. If three signals be given in answer, then say, 'If I speak the letters of the alphabet slowly, will you signal every time I come to the letter you want, and spell us out a message?' Should three signals be given, set to work on the plan proposed, and from this time an intelligent system of communication is established.

"8. Afterward the question should be put

'Are we sitting in the right order to get the best manifestations?' Probably some members of the circle will then be told to change seats with each other, and the signals will be afterward strengthened. Next ask, 'Who is the medium?' When spirits come asserting themselves to be related or known to any one present, well-chosen questions should be put to test the accuracy of the statements, as spirits out of the body have all the virtues and all the failings of spirits in the body." *

"Always have a slate, or pen, pencil and paper on the table, so as not to be obliged to rise and procure them. Especially avoid all entering or quitting the room, moving about, irrelevant conversation, or disturbances within or without the circle room, after the seance has once commenced.

"The spirits are far more punctual to seasons, faithful to promise, and periodical in action, than mortals. Endeavor, then, to fix your cir-

---

* James H. Young : " Rules and Advice to Circles," page 6.

cle at a convenient hour, when you will be least interrupted, and do not fail in your appointments. Do not admit unpunctual, late comers, or, if possible, suffer the air of the room to be disturbed in any way after the sitting commences. Nothing but necessity, indisposition, or impressions (to be hereafter described), should warrant the least disturbance of the sitting, WHICH SHOULD NEVER EXCEED TWO HOURS, unless an extension of time be solicited of the spirits. Let the seance always extend to one hour, even if no results are obtained. It sometimes requires all that time for the spirits to form their battery from the materials furnished. Let it also be remembered that all circles are experimental; hence no one should be discouraged if phenomena are not produced at the first few sittings. Stay with the same circle for six sittings: if no phenomena are then produced (provided all the above conditions are observed), you may be sure that you are not rightly assimilated to each other—you do not form the requisite

LAWS OF THE SPIRIT CIRCLE.

combinations, or neutralize each other. In that case, break up, and let a portion of the members of your circle meet with other persons. That is, change one, two, or three members of your circle for others, and keep changing them, if necessary, until you succeed.

"A well-developed test-medium may sit without injury for any person, or any description of character or temperament; but a circle sitting for mutual development should never admit persons addicted to bad habits, criminals, sensualists. or strongly positive persons of any kind, whether rude, skeptical, violent-tempered or dogmatical.

"An humble, candid, inquiring spirit, unprejudiced, and receptive of truth, possesses the only proper frame of mind in which to sit for phenomena, the delicate magnetism of which is shaped, tempered, and made or marred as much by mental as physical conditions. When once any of the circle can communicate freely and conclusively with spirits, the spirits can and will take charge of and regulate the future movements of the circle."*

While the foregoing rules may be beneficial to those who are seeking light upon this subject, I would not advise a novice to begin his researches into spirit matters by joining an immature circle. Nor would I recommend or encourage the forming of such circles, without the assistance of a reliable medium, or some person who is conversant with the laws through which manifestations commonly occur. The process of development through the crude circle alone is altogether too slow for this lively age. Ninety-nine per cent. of spiritual beginners become exhausted and abandon the project long before they reach results at all satisfactory.

A developing circle may be formed in almost any family, and some slight progress towards unlocking the future, without the aid of mature media, may be attained; but such a

* Emma Hardinge.

method of inquiry is about as impracticable as the attempt to conduct a district school without the aid of a competent teacher.

CHAPTER IV.

OBSTACLES TO BE ENCOUNTERED.

PERHAPS there is no better method of acquainting the investigator with the obstacles he is sure to encounter in the study of spirit phenomena, than the recital of a portion of my own experience. During the winter of 1856–7 I began to investigate the subject of spiritualism by accepting an invitation to attend a spirit circle held in my neighborhood, where the alleged phenomena were chiefly confined to spirit-rappings and table-tippings. I was seated in a circle composed of eight ladies and gentlemen, and surrounding a common dining-table. The medium, a well-known lady, whose honesty I had never before questioned, sat directly opposite me. A few songs were sung, and perhaps an hour was passed very pleasantly, but without result—when, of a sudden, the table began slowly to waver and I felt my side of it rising. I was not a little surprised, for, to confess the truth, I had come more than half prepared to disbelieve my own senses; consequently I began to look about me very critically for the cause of the marvel. It was not long before I discovered, by the unnaturally white appearance of the lady medium's finger-nails, thé unmistakable evidence that she was bearing heavily upon the opposite side of the table. A few questions were asked by members of the circle, without very satisfactory results, however, when the phenomena changed, and several slight raps were heard, which apparently proceeded from a point directly under the hands of the medium. Again I was on the alert, and again I thought I detected her in producing the raps by cautiously working the tips of her fingers along the varnished surface of the table, as well as by pressing the nail of her folded thumb against a short pencil held perpendicularly. A few names of recognized departed spirits were spelled out by the raps, when the circle closed. I left the house that evening in disgust, and, without stopping to meditate upon the truths that had been developed, without asking the medium whether the movements I detected were voluntary or involuntary, or whether she was mentally responsible during the entire sitting, I boldly declared to my comrades that the medium in question was an impostor—that I had detected her, and that was the end of it. Of course, I was unanimously ruled out of that circle, and consequently lost the whole winter's development.

Had I exercised better judgment, and strictly obeyed the required conditions by remaining passive all the time, no doubt I would have made great progress in my investigations during that winter, instead of retrograding as I did; for the lady in question afterward became one of the most celebrated mediums in the country. My conduct is, however, but a fair illustration of the manner of investigation pursued by the average beginner. The novice is usually critical, skeptical, and exacting, invariably looking for fraud instead of fact. All testimony in spiritual matters is worthless until the investigator has been a long time in the field of research and has become acquainted with the more important laws by which spirit power operates upon ponderable substances. When the spirits desire to move a table, they must use the best means at their command; since they cannot always create favorable conditions, they are frequently forced to employ means which, to those ignorant of spirit rules, may appear fraudulent, but which, in reality, are established and unalterable laws. Allan Kardec, one of the most reliable writers upon this subject, says:

"When a table is moved under your hands, the spirit evoked draws from the universal fluid what animates the table with factious life. The table thus prepared, the spirit attracts it and moves it under the influence of his own fluid, thrown off by his will. When the mass he wishes to move is too heavy for him, he calls to his aid spirits who are in the same condition as himself. By reason of his ethereal nature, the spirit proper cannot act upon gross matter without intermediary assistance, that is to say, without the link that unites it to matter. This link, which we call *Périsprit*, gives the key to all material spirit phenomena."

Thus it is often the case that, at a crude circle, largely composed of skeptics and weak media, the spirits become impatient, and, being too anxious to encourage the sitters, or to close the circle, act rashly and unwisely, and make a direct attack upon the medium, before developing their *périsprit*. In such cases the medium, it is claimed, becomes wholly irresponsible, being simply a tool in the power of the spirits ; and through his unconscious physical man they are enabled to act upon inanimate matter. This fact, that MEDIUMS ARE NOT ALWAYS RESPONSIBLE FOR THEIR ACTIONS, is one of the first important lessons that the investigator should learn.

Involuntary Muscular Action.—Physiology teaches us that the movement of many muscles in the human body, like those acting upon the heart and stomach, are wholly involuntary ; that others, such as those controlling respiration, the movements of the eye, etc., work involuntarily, but may be partially controlled ; while the movements of the hands, legs, and many other portions of the body, are wholly subject to the will-power of the individual. There are times, however, in every person's life, during trance, deep sleep, protracted illness, and the like, when the action of the whole body becomes involuntary. Thus the spirits, as it is claimed by the best authority, often act upon mediums in such a manner as to cause them to appear dishonest, when, in reality, they are furnishing the very best and most cogent evidences of spirit power.

CHAPTER V.

"PÉRISPRIT."

THE existence of a subtile and supposed to be immeasurable force, like the *périsprit*, referred to by Kardec, has been known, and publicly recognized by some of our most intelligent spiritual writers, for many years. But little, however, has been known, until quite recently, of its true character, or the exact method by which it may be produced. As late as 1871, Thomas R. Hazard, one of the best informed writers on this subject, refers to the *périsprit* in the following communication, received from the spirit world, which shows how little was then known of its character or potency, even by our spirit friends themselves. I quote his language *verbatim:*

"I learned from Mr. Luther Colby that, at a recent private seance given by Mrs. Annie Lord Chamberlain, at the rooms of Mrs. J. H. Conant, 76 Waltham street, Boston, the following answer was received from a spirit-guide of the medium, to the question, 'By what process do the invisibles materialize the hands, faces, and other forms that from time to time are shown at circles held for physical demonstration of spirit power?'

"The influence controlling at the time replied that the refined matter out of which these apparitions were formed—or at least rendered cognizable by mortal senses—was gathered from the individuals composing the circle, each contributing to the supply. The raw material was then collected together in a mass—as the housewife, having kneaded the dough for bread, prepares it to be rolled out into any form desired—and a certain portion (sufficient for the manifestations about to be made) divided from it. This portion, by the subtle force of spirit chemistry, was deposited in solution in a vapor, or atmospheric, bath over the heads of the circle, just as the copper is held in solution in the bath of the battery for electrotyping. Immediately the spirit-hand, or other object, is plunged in the bath, and, as is the case with the copper upon the plate in the process above referred to, the earthly matter in solution becomes precipitated upon the surface of the spirit object to be shown, and the form thus coated with said earthly material becomes tangible and visible to physical senses."

Again, the same writer says that a spirit purporting to be that of the notorious Captain Kidd, came through one Gilbert D. Eaton, a trance medium from Rochester, and declared that

" The limbs and faces that are shown undergo a chemical process, analogous to that adopted by mortals in coating or galvanizing specimens of wood, or other substances, and metals, with the wash of another kind of metal ; that this material coating for the spirit form is collected by the spirits, and partially prepared during the dark circle, from the *aura* or effete particles that are constantly passing from the human body—the cold breeze that is so often felt by the persons present being a part of it: and that the consistency or efficiency of the material depends upon the degree of harmony that prevails in the circle.

"He further stated that these effete particles cannot be used by the spirit chemists that preside over and direct the operations at Moravia, (of whom Franklin is one of the chief), until they are vitalized so as to make them partake of the quality of living flesh; and, to do this, it is necessary to pass them *through*, or bring them in *contact* with, a human organism possessing certain properties such as appertain to Mrs. Andrews, who always sits under the aperture during the process of collecting, preparing and passing the material into the cabinet. Mr. Eaton's controlling spirit also asserted that the manufacturing of this occult material requires that certain elements should be abstracted from every organ of the medium; and that, on some

"*PERISPRIT.*"

occasions, where the manifestations required high coloring, the spirit artists had drawn as many as four ounces of actual blood from her veins."

From the foregoing communications, it is evident that the spirits in control were of the same opinion as many scientists in the physical form, who then supposed that the *aura*, or *périsprit*, was generated and used only at materializing circles. More recent discoveries, however, reveal the fact that this subtile force forms an *indispensable factor in all circles* where spirit manifestations are allowed to occur. The latest information upon this subject was disclosed to the material world within the last few weeks by one of my most trustworthy spirit-guides, who says:

This ethereal property is so light and volatile, and at the same time so powerful, that enough might be generated at a single sitting, by a complete circle, to fertilize every seance on earth, provided it could be properly diffused; and, yet, this vast quantity, when first produced, would scarcely fill a one-eighth ounce vial. Probably no substance yet known to the material or spiritual world can be compared with it in the matter of attenuation. An ounce of gold, it is said, can be drawn out so fine that it will make a wire reaching fifty miles, and can be battered so thin that leaves of it will float upon the very air. A single grain of musk will perfume a room for years, thereby showing its wonderful volatile properties. But even these ductile and ethereal substances are among the crudest of the crude when compared with the *périsprit*.

"Another property of the *périsprit* which pertains to its ethereal nature, is penetrability. Matter is no obstacle; it passes through everything, as the light passes through transparent bodies."*

Thus far there has been an immense loss of energy connected with the development of this remarkable fluid. At an ordinary circle, but

* Allan Kardec on Mediums, page 141.

an infinitesimal portion of the amount generated can be utilized, while the remainder passes off and is lost. But at the Great Head-center Chemical Laboratory of the spirit-world, they are now perfecting, and expect soon to have in full operation, an apparatus by which they will be enabled to save the *périsprit* as it is generated, and store it up for future use. Already the spirits have established a table of weights and measures by which it may be estimated. The unit of measurement is designated by the word "finitesimal," which means the one-thousandth part of the product of an hour's sitting by a complete circle of eight persons, "representing equi-force, positive and negative." This amount of *périsprit* can easily be so attenuated that it will form a belt seven feet wide, reaching seven times around the earth. Unlike any other substance known either to the physical or spiritual world, the potency of the *périsprit* increases as it is dilated, in the same proportion that a falling body gathers momentum in its descent. The highest point of its attenuation yet known has been accomplished at the Royal Æsthetical Chemical Laboratory of Spiritual Science, where it is generated, dilated and diffused for the express use of trance-speakers and Indian spirit-guides. In this laboratory the *périsprit* becomes so tenuous and transparent that the eleven-millionth part of one "finitesimal" will so inspire the crudest and most ignorant medium as to bring him to his feet for an hour's talk.

CHAPTER VI.

THE DIAKKA.

ANOTHER source of annoyance to the investigator, probably the greatest stumbling-block among all the spiritual obstacles he has to encounter, is the Diakka.

This monster, it is claimed, has done more to injure the cause of Spiritualism than have all other evils combined. Yet, he is a necessary influence, forming such an important factor therein, that it is difficult even to imagine the existence of a spiritual system without him.

The spirit of James Victor Wilson, through his medium, Andrew Jackson Davis, says:

"The Diakka is a spirit who takes insane delight in playing parts, in juggling tricks, in personating opposite characters; to whom prayers and profane utterances are of equi-value; surcharged with a passion for lyrical narrations; one whose every attitude is instinct with the schemes of specious reasoning, sophistry, pride, pleasure, wit, subtle convivialities; a boundless disbeliever, one who thinks that all private life will end in the all-consuming self-love of God. He is an unbalanced, not always an evil, person; he wanders in his own congenial forest, never resting, never satisfied with life; after amusing himself with jugglery and tricky witticisms, invariably victimizing others—secretly tormenting mediums, causing them to exaggerate in speech, and to falsify by acts; unlocking and unbolting the street doors of your memory; pointing your feet into wrong paths, and far more. Nevertheless, the good physicians of love, and the ministers of truth, labor among the Diakka (the angel women, as missionaries, far exceed the men); so that in time each and all are reached and delivered from the dense wilderness of discord into which circumstances and a voluntary yielding to wrong inclinations primarily consigned them."

Referring to the Diakka at a subsequent sitting, Andrew Jackson Davis, while not under influence, writes as follows:

"I but obey my impression, indorsed by the best conclusion of my reason, when I affirm what by observation I have been long familiar with, that a very large proportion of *discordant* and *repulsive* and *false* experiences in Spiritualism are to be explained by admitting into your hypothesis a *fact*, namely: that the Diakka are continually victimizing sensitive persons, making sport of them, and having a jolly laughing-time at the expense of really honest and sincere people, including mediums, whom they especially take delight in psychologizing and dispossessing of the use of will. There is no kind of alleged obsession, no species of assumed witchcraft, no phase of religious insanity where such psychology is not possible. The remedy consists in the knowledge. Remove the mystery of spiritual intercourse, and you remove the danger. No person of ordinary judgment, with *will* enough to draw a pail of water, or to walk a mile up hill, need complain that he cannot overcome the influence of a Diakka. They, at most, can do nothing more than confuse your thoughts, break up the lines of your memory, mingle their inclinations with your own, and psychologize your nervous and muscular systems. If you yield, in your moments of curiosity or when morally weak, you cannot escape legitimate punishment. If you walk one mile with your enemy, he will try to force you to go twain; gratify his trifling impertinence for thirty minutes, and he may try to exhibit you as a fool to your neighbors the ensuing thirty days. Beware of the first false step."

It is claimed by some materialists that the Diakka is an imaginary personage, a fungus, or mere outgrowth, of Spiritualism;

that the times demanded him, and he came ; that he is to Spiritualism what a personal devil is to the creed of the orthodox religionists. Without the Diakka and his Satanic majesty both systems would inevitably fall to the ground. Necessity being the mother of invention, Christians are freely credited with the paternity of the one, while Andrew Jackson Davis is pointed out as the putative father of the other. Neither supposition can, however, be true. The latter is particularly erroneous from a materialistic standpoint, since it is only reasonable to suppose that a father must be older than his son.

The following ancient record will show that the Diakka is not an infant, or even a new-comer among us, but had existed and exerted his influence over mankind for ages before the advent of either Christianity or modern Spiritualism. In the twenty-second chapter of I. Kings, the workings of the Diakka are very minutely described.

It seems that Ahab, one of the kings of Israel, who had sold himself to work wickedness in the sight of the Lord, at the instigation of his wife, Jezebel, had a great desire to own Ramoth-gilead, which belonged to the king of Syria. So he called upon Jehoshaphat, the king of Judah (4th verse), "And he said unto Jehoshaphat, Wilt thou go with me to battle Ramoth-gilead? And Jehoshaphat said to the king of Israel, I am as thou art, my people as thy people, my horses as thy horses. . . . Enquire, I pray thee, at the word of the Lord to-day." Then the king called together about four hundred prophets, and they said, "Go up, for the Lord shall deliver it into the hand of the king." But Jehoshaphat was not yet convinced that he would be justified in making war on his own kin, so he inquired: "Is there not here a prophet of the Lord besides, that we might enquire of him?" And Ahab said: "There is yet one man, Micaiah, the son of Imlah, by whom we may enquire of the Lord; but I hate him; for he doth not prophesy good concerning me, but evil." But, at the urgent request of Jehoshaphat, the king sent a messenger to Micaiah, which messenger tried to persuade him to prophesy just as the other four hundred prophets had done. "And Micaiah said, As the Lord liveth, what the Lord saith unto me, that will I speak." Now, it appears that the Lord was displeased with the wicked king, and Jezebel, his wife, and wished to destroy them both; so when Micaiah came to the king, he advised him to go to battle against Ramoth-gilead, saying: "Go and prosper, for the Lord shall deliver it into the hand of the king." But the king had received a premonition, or spirit warning, that the battle would go against him, and did not believe what Micaiah said. "And the king said unto him, How many times shall I adjure thee that thou tell me nothing but that which is true in the name of the Lord?" Then Micaiah acknowledged that he and the four hundred other prophets had given a false prophecy, saying: "I saw all Israel scattered upon the hills, as sheep that have not a shepherd; and the Lord said, These have no master: let them return, every man to his house in peace."

"And the king of Israel said unto Jehoshaphat, Did I not tell thee that he would prophesy no good concerning me, but evil?

"And he said, Hear, thou, therefore, the word of the Lord: I saw the Lord sitting on his throne, and all the host of heaven standing by him, on his right hand and on his left.

"And the Lord said, Who shall persuade Ahab, that he may go up and fall at Ramoth-gilead? And one said on this manner, and another said on that manner.

"And there came forth a spirit, and stood before the Lord, and said, I will persuade him.

"And the Lord said unto him, Wherewith? And he said, I will go forth and I will be a *lying spirit*, in the mouth of all his prophets. And he said, Thou shalt persuade him, and prevail also; go forth, and do so.

"Now, therefore, behold, the Lord hath put a lying spirit in the mouth of all these thy prophets, and the Lord hath spoken evil concerning thee."

And the king was right, for, notwithstanding he disguised himself, by changing his raiment, and taking every other precaution which he could devise, he was wounded on the battle-field, and died that same night, directly in the face of the predictions of the four hundred prophets, who spoke under control of Diakka, or lying spirits.

CHAPTER VII.

THE HOME OF THE DIAKKA.

WHEN not engaged in earthly duties, the Diakka usually remains in his enchanting home, denominated the great "Draco Major Belt." This celestial wilderness is located several billions of miles distant from the earth, and occupies the whole sphere of the southwestern heavens. Its magnitude and beauties are minutely described by the spirit of a profound and accurate mathematician, James Victor Wilson, who has been permitted to visit that wonderful locality, and who subsequently made a partial survey of the belt, reporting to Andrew Jackson Davis as follows :

"This wonderful country of the Diakka excites your unenlightened fancy, first, by its mighty wealth of magnitude, and, second, by the wonderful character of its aerial crown, over the shadow of the enchained trapezium, mottled with delicate brilliant points, so dazzlingly bright and exquisitely prismatic as to make the immediate surroundings black, giving the beholder an impression that the hills and dales and forests beneath must be insufferably splendid with diamonds and golden riches too perfect for earthly eyes to gaze upon. Intense, central globular lights, softened rapidly into frames of perfect globes of blackness, but with very jagged and broken outline, appearing and disappearing under the eye, sometimes in bars and lines of incalculable length, at other times at irregular intervals and with the free variety of order, almost complete chaos, peculiar to the appearance of stars and the constellations visible at night from earth in different parts of the sky.

" Reverting for a moment to its magnitude (supposing it were a complete belt of country, instead of only a third in the form of a semi-circle) it would require not less than one million eight hundred and three thousand and twenty-six diameters of the earth to measure the longitudinal extent of the celestial wilderness."

A later, and, as I claim, more accurate report from the Diakka land, was recently given to me by my own control, or spirit-guide, MUHLENBURG, who had just returned from an extended exploration and survey of that apparently boundless wilderness. He informs me that Mr. Wilson's description refers only to a portion of the great "Draco Major Belt," comprising about one-fifth of its entire area. MUHLENBURG has discovered that this celestial belt forms a complete circle, extending away beyond our planetary system. So vast are the dimensions of this region, that the measurement of its diameter not only defies all our powers of mensuration, but quite transcends those of the human imagination. Not only do the Diakka of the earth inhabit this belt, but it is the home of untold billions of spirits from planets of other suns.

CHAPTER VIII.

MARY ANDREWS, THE MORAVIA MEDIUM.

IN November, 1871, I paid a visit to the above medium, with the purpose to investigate the manifestations said to occur through her agency. Upon my return home, I prepared the following article, which was published in the *Syracuse Journal:*

"Having noticed, from time to time, in many of the leading newspapers of this State, accounts of so-called spiritual manifestations now taking place at the house of Morris Keeler, near the village of Moravia, in Cayuga county your correspondent was prevailed upon, a short time since, to make a visit to that locality, in order to witness the new and startling apparitions that have so recently been presented to mortals from the spirit world. The location of this famous house, and the history of the occupants, have been so often given by other writers that it will be unnecessary for me to present a particular description of them. Morris Keeler, the owner of this haunted house, is a very credulous and illiterate man, about sixty years of age, who conducts all of his business affairs, as he informs us, according to the direction of departed spirits. Every morning, he receives instructions for the day, through his adopted daughter, Mrs. Andrews, the celebrated medium, who has made his home so notorious. With a keen eye to business and finance, the spirits, about one year ago, turned this old man's house into a hotel, capable of accommodating about twenty guests at a time. Fifty cents a meal, or two dollars per day, is the regular price for board. All other accommodations are extra. Mrs. Andrews is a coarse-featured, uneducated woman, about thirty years of age. She does business on her own account, charging, invariably, two dollars per sitting, which amount is usually made up by the gentle-

THE MORAVIA MEDIUM. 65

men present. On making our business known to the medium, we were informed that she had already given five seances since morning, to a large number of people, and the spirits had so "drawed" on her that it would be impossible for us to get a satisfactory sitting until the next day. Accordingly, at an early hour on the following day, I found myself, in company with six or eight other individuals, seated in the spirits' room.

We were placed in a semi-circle by Mr. Keeler, the "boss" of ceremonies, who informed us that we must all join hands, keep our feet on the floor, keep close to the chairs in which we were sitting, and in no circumstances allow the circle to be broken. The medium soon came in, dressed as we had seen her before, except she had a large water-proof cloak thrown over her shoulders and wore a pair of loose slippers on her feet, and seated herself within the semi-circle, about six feet from each person present. The lights were now extinguished and we found ourselves in total darkness.

‘

Nothing transpired for ten or fifteen minutes, when the medium broke the awful silence by directing us to sing, or the spirits could do "nothin'." A lively tune was finally started by a part of the company, when two beautiful, tiny phosphorescent lights were seen dancing about within the circle. Several notes of the piano were touched, and some of the party felt spirit hands laid on their heads, etc., etc. Everything was progressing finely when, unfortunately, the medium, or some spirit clothed in material form, ran against your correspondent's foot, which he had carelessly thrust out into the circle in violation of the required conditions. The lights disappeared in an instant and everything was still. In a few seconds, a stentorian voice called out: "Down with your feet!" I apologized for being so thoughtless, but did not remove my foot from where it was, and had been through all the performance. As soon as the spirits were satisfied that everything was in working order again, demonstrations were renewed —water was sprinkled in our faces, the backs of our hands were touched, another light was seen floating about in the air until, again, some clumsy spirit ran over your correspondent's foot, when two raps on the floor were distinctly heard, which Mr. Keeler informed us were the closing manifestations of seance number one. After resting for an hour or two, we re-assembled in the spirit-room, with several new members added to our circle. All of the company were invited to inspect the cabinet, which consisted of one part of the room separated from the circle by a plain board partition, containing a small aperture about eight by twelve inches square, and perhaps four and a half feet from the floor. Over this small opening hung a black curtain. Nothing remarkable was discovered in this apartment, except by one gentleman, who picked up a small ringlet from the floor, which he suggested the spirits had, in their hasty flight, neglected to transform into spirit hair. As soon as we had vacated the cabinet, Mrs. Andrews deliberately walked into it, and, seating herself in a chair, requested Mr. Keeler to shut and fasten the door, as she desired to be alone with the spirits. No one presumed to interfere with the medium by asking impertinent questions, nor did any one present seem to care how many false faces, wigs, whiskers, and other paraphernalia, she might have concealed under her immense water-proof cloak; but every one seemed too anxious to witness all that the most favorable conditions could produce. A lamp was placed in one corner of the room, so shaded that only a faint light falling directly on the opening was visible. After waiting anxiously for a quarter of an hour or so, the black curtain was quickly drawn aside by some invisible hand, and a face appeared at the aperture for an instant and vanished. Several similar faces were presented without being recognized, when a female figure, with long gray hair and an old-fashioned cap on the head, was seen for a second, which was fully recognized by one of the party as his grandmother, who had been dead for over twenty years. When questioned by some one of the company as to her identity, this individual gravely informed us that he was positive—*he knew his grandmother by the number of ruffles she had on her cap.* This evidence seemed to be entirely satisfactory to all present! The next face that presented itself appeared to be that of a young man with black hair and a long, dark mustache. At first, no one seemed to recognize this face, when, finally, a skeptical individual from Syracuse remarked that it might be the spirit of Mr. B. (B. was a man over seventy years of age when he left this world, whose hair was as white as snow.) I replied, "If this is the spirit of B., he must have shaved off his long *black* whiskers." Immediately the figure re-appeared, fully answering the latter description of B.; but our Syracuse friend, not being as yet fully satisfied, inquired, in a tone just loud enough to be heard by the medium, if Mr. B. had not lost two fingers from his right hand. To our surprise, in a few seconds, the required right hand, with two fingers bent down out of sight, was seen slowly passing by the aperture. Five or ten minutes elapsed, when the spirits, speaking through a huge tin horn, directed us to sing. An effort was made by some of the company to comply with this request, but singing did not seem to be our forte, whereupon one gentleman informed the company that the spirits wanted harmony of thought and concentration of action, and suggested spatting of hands in lieu of singing. This experiment proved entirely successful. The spirits, forgetting that the circle had been broken by this new dodge, proceeded to show us demonstrations fully equal to anything that we had before witnessed.

This remarkable seance was concluded by a fifteen minutes' speech, through the tin horn, by some unknown spirit, whose peculiar accent and ungrammatical language, did not seem strange to any one acquainted with the medium. When we reflect upon the fact that these flimsy tests are among the strongest which can be produced by this notorious medium to prove the existence of departed spirits and their oral communication with the living, and that this woman is sustained in her deception by such great spirit-lights as Charles Foster, of New York, and others high in the "profession," we cannot help feeling mortified at the credulity of innocent believers, and disgusted with the conduct of those who could perpetrate such a fraud.

When the foregoing attempted exposure was made, I was not a believer in spiritual apparitions, or spirit manifestations of any kind; consequently I was neither an impartial, nor an unprejudiced witness. Yet my report of what occurred was correctly given in every particular. I described only what I thought I saw, felt and heard, precisely as it appeared to

me. Owing to my entire ignorance of th[e]
laws governing materializing circles, at th[e]
time, I have no doubt that I mistook the wor[d]
of the Diakka, through the unconscious bod[y]
of the medium, for her own individual act[s.]
Since, however, I have learned more of th[e]
science of Spiritualism, that which the[n]
appeared to me mysterious and frauduler[t]
now invests itself with the unmistakabl[e]
attributes of truth.

To-day, I feel that an apology is due Mr[s.]
Andrews for my share in her early failures.
attended her circle—as I have since bee[n]
informed by my control—in such a frame [of]
mind that I attracted a large number of Diakk[a]
who quite overpowered her, for the expre[ss]
purpose of making it appear to me that sh[e]
was an impostor. Again, while sitting in th[e]
circle, I did not strictly adhere to the require[d]
conditions, but listened to the suggestions of
Diakka who said, "Keep your feet well o[ut]
into the circle, so as to trip the medium.[″]
Then the same spirits, as I have since bee[n]

informed by my spirit-guides, approached Mrs. Andrews, and, putting her into a semi-unconscious state, caused her to walk over my feet—thus giving the color of literal truth to my report. Instead, however, of disproving the action of the spirits (when all the facts are known), this very act assists in demonstrating their power. Again, when I saw the two little stars, or phosphorescent lights, just far enough apart to be reached by the outstretched arms of the medium, I knew, what my guides have since told me was true, that she produced them by holding a common lucifer-match between the thumb and finger of each hand, and that, after moistening them a little, she could cause the lights to appear and disappear, by simply opening and closing her hands. But I did not then know, as I have since learned, that the spirits impelled her to do all this, and that she herself was not responsible for her actions, but was an unwilling tool in their hands.

When I heard her coarse, ungrammatical

language uttered through the tin horn, which
I readily recognized, by her peculiar pronunci-
ation of certain words, I was unacquainted
with the laws governing "dead control," and
honestly believed that she was voluntarily and
deliberately speaking, when, in reality, the
voice was that of a Mr. Butler, formerly of
Syracuse, N. Y., who had been murdered, and
who was strong enough, at the time, to take
dead control of the medium, although not able
to disguise her voice, or correct her phraseol-
ogy. When we all felt the whole house tremble, for a few minutes, while the medium was
outside the cabinet, I knew, what has since
been confirmed by my spirit-guides, that Mary
Andrews stood well away from the side walls
of the room, upon a spot where the joists were
weak, and, by rapidly raising and lowering herself upon her toes, so that her heels would not
quite touch the floor, the whole house was
made to vibrate very perceptibly: but I was
not sufficiently familiar with the laws governing materialization to comprehend that, owing

to the condition of the circle, and the presence of a number of skeptics, there was not sufficient force to generate the *périsprit*—consequently the spirits were obliged to employ Mrs. Andrews to shake the house for them, in the manner I have described. When I saw a figure at the aperture, purporting to be the materialized spirit of a very near and dear relative, who is yet alive, my mind was filled with doubt, which soon ripened into a firm belief that the medium was a gross impostor, who made her living by preying upon the credulity of weak-minded people; hence I felt justified in reporting her as a mere empiric. Since, however, I have become more familiar with the details of the science, I have made the spiritual acquaintance of thousands of Diakka, and I can easily account for all that took place upon a purely spiritual hypothesis. I do not therefore, hesitate to declare, in this public manner, that if there is such a creature in existence as a genuine materializing medium, MARY ANDREWS is one.

When Mr. William White, then editor of the "Banner of Light," in the presence of myself and a venerated friend, picked up, from the floor of the cabinet, a blonde curl, which Mrs. Andrews had evidently used in the decoration of one of her materialized spirit-friends, and we all laughed as we talked the matter over, Mr. White declaring that "*it looked pretty thin,*" I honestly believed that we had exposed the medium, when, in fact, we had only revealed our own ignorance. And it was not until after Mr. White returned to Boston, and published in his paper a glowing account of a seance given by Mrs. Andrews, in which the writer indorsed the medium as genuine, that I awoke to the fact that a spirit has just as good a right to wear false hair as any one who is yet in the flesh. When a figure appeared in the cabinet, answering to the name of my venerable friend Mr. B., and exhibiting a long, black beard, I did not know that it was a Diakka playing a trick upon me, and that I was the victim of my own prejudice. To show the great contrast between the report of a novice like myself, who was entirely ignorant of nearly all the laws governing spiritual circles, and the report of one who had been converted to the glorious cause, and could see with a clearer vision, I append an account written by Thomas R. Hazard, who passed eleven days at Moravia, witnessing the same manifestations, through the same medium, only a short time after I had left :

"Upon my arrival, on the 27th of December, 1871, at Mr. Keeler's, I found but three or four visitors there, including a Mr. Livingston, who resided not many miles away, and Mrs. Kate Gibbs, of Utica, N. Y., both of them highly mediumistic, and friends of the family, and familiar with the phenomena that usually occur. At the first seance, held on the afternoon of the 27th, the manifestations were weak and unsatisfactory, both in the dark and light circle. At the latter, two male faces appeared at the same time, but were too indistinct to be recognized or described. I was told by those present, that, for several weeks past, the power had been daily decreasing and apparently dying out. Mr. Keeler himself told me that he was not expecting the usual manifestations to continue, as the *spirits* were about making a change. Mrs. Andrews, the medium, seemed also downhearted and discouraged, and I began to fear that the object of my visit to Moravia would prove a failure.

"Before leaving New York, I had two sittings with Mrs. Staats, 53 East 20th street, at which my wife and two daughters came, among others, and reiterated their intention (as before conveyed through the mediumship of Mrs. Rockwood, 14 East Springfield street, Boston) of showing themselves to me at Moravia. My daughter Anna [who passed away in early womanhood] told me she meant to hand me a a lily [her favorite flower when in earth-life]. The communications made through Mrs. Staats were in writing, which I read and put in my valise, not knowing that I should ever refer to them again; but, on learning the state of things at Moravia, I re-read them, and was surprised to find how nearly some of the statements they contained tallied with what I found existing there—especially two communications purporting to emanate from the spirit of Theodore Parker, extracts from which I give below, word for word, exactly as written by the hand of Mrs. Staats, December 14th and 21st, 1878:

"'My friend, I promise you, if you will remain to join the circle which will gather, to add another crowning proof to your faith. We know that you have the attracting power, and all we ask is the time. There are so many going there, that, as you are well aware, the place requires some change of magnetism, and the medium some instruction. Men and women who go entirely out of curiosity are very apt to carry with them an adulterated magnetism, which leaves sometimes an odor and a sphere very disagreeable to a more advanced spirit. The wonder is, that it has run so. long as it has without an entire break-up. The medium seldom has a person sit down with her who regards her with the slightest degree of humanity. Indeed, they hold her responsible for all disappointments that may arise, and expect from her the greater manifestation from the fact of their unbelief. We desire to have you give her some encouragement; and we ask, also, that you remain as long as possible, making some suggestions, which we will give you, to improve the condition of affairs there. The fact is, the medium is already in a transition state, and the control are undecided whether to remove or increase the manifestations. I want the cabinet simplified and made more convenient; for, as these manifestations increase there, they will spread everywhere, and the result will be spirits talking face to face with man. I see great advancement and earnest investigation everywhere. One thing is certain: nothing else can make man a law to himself and a light to others, and there is but one thing to look for progress in, namely: individual reform—learning to think and act for one's self. I will not interfere with your family circle, but will show myself, if possible to you.' . . .

"At a second sitting, December 21st, the same spirit said: 'I come with you, my friend, to-night, and am well pleased to meet you. I come to offer our congratulations, and ask you to go forward in the path of progress, being bold in the truth. The time has arrived when all material things point to a verification of what was told you so long ago The great struggles for truth are still going on, the conflict still being waged : and heaven and earth are acting in concert to produce to man the proper evidences of life immortal. Your articles have made a better basis for mediums, and opened the way for us to do our work better. We ask that you go to Moravia. We promise to meet you there, and will talk face to face with you. Do not allow anything to interfere with you. Go alone, and be prepared to wait a few days, at least. Do not be hastened away, nor let those come in with you who are in any way

disagreeable. We shall advise your going in what we call the holiday week, for the reason that most persons will be at home at that time, and there will be less confusion there. In finishing this, we will give you a list of who will meet you there; and we ask that you throw off all external care, and wait patiently until we come. We promise, and will perform. DANIEL WEBSTER.
THEODORE PARKER."

Here the control was suddenly broken by an interruption.

"Both before going and whilst at Moravia, I frequently remarked that I had seen and heard enough to satisfy me beyond doubt of a future state of existence, and that the object of my visit was not so much to obtain any new light for my own satisfaction as for others; believing that, if I could see a spirit face so clearly as to be willing to affirm to its identity, it might be the means of causing some others to break away from the trammels of early education and habit, and investigate the subject for themselves. I was therefore careful to say nothing to compromise my object; and, further than the bestowal of a few words of encouragement and sympathy upon the medium, I said nothing, until several days after my arrival at Moravia, in connection with the foregoing spirit communications.

"On the next day, the 28th, the manifestations were somewhat better, both in the dark and light circles, than they had been, as was said, for some weeks. A daughter of Mr. Livingston—who died in very early infancy— came and delivered quite a lengthy and highly instructive discourse. Several hands and arms were plainly exhibited, both outside and immediately within the cabinet, some of which were acknowledged as my wife's and daughter's. What purported to be my own mother, showed herself so that I could clearly see her plain Quaker bonnet, with cap beneath, but not her face distinctly enough to recognize it. Others present—whose eyesight was stronger than mine—described the features, however, as very much resembling hers. She also spoke audibly for a minute or two, very sensibly and characteristically, but not in her natural voice, but like one speaking through a trumpet— which might have been the case, as her face was not visible whilst speaking. Although I felt no doubt of her identity, and so expressed myself, she seemed disappointed that I could not see her more plainly, and made repeated efforts to bring her face further forward into the light. [I regretted that I had not brought an opera-glass with me, which might have assisted my vision.]

"On the forenoon of the next day, the 29th, my mother showed herself again in the same bonnet and cap, but I was still unable to distinguish her features so as to recognize them, although I had no doubt, as before, of her identity. Several new-comers had joined this morning circle, and among them G. E. Hoyt, of Chicago, who seemed to possess a magnetism wonderfully attractive to spirits. At this seance, several of his deceased relatives and friends showed themselves plainly, and conversed intelligently with him. I question whether there were any persons present who doubted their individual identity, though it would require a volume to describe the various shades and phases of phenomena that occur at only one of these sittings, so as to make them intelligible to readers who have never witnessed the manifestations.

" I have before stated that, at a seance held with Mrs. Staats, in New York, a few days before I went to Moravia, my daughter Anna said she would hand me a lily whilst I was there. I also find, by reference to a memorandum, that my wife assured me, whilst at Mrs. Rockwood's, in Boston, on the 9th of last November, that she felt confident she and our two daughters, Anna and Mary, would be able to show themselves to me at Moravia, entwined in each other's arms, the last-named characteristically wreathed or garlanded with flowers. On inspecting the cabinet at Moravia I saw, at the first glance, that the aperture would not admit of such a manifestation as this; but the circumstance did not disconcert me in the least, having learned through experience that the spirits of mortals are—except in degree—no more infallible or omniscient in one sphere of existence than in another.

"The hands and arms that were shown at the aperture, unlike the faces, were always plain and distinct. On an occasion early after my arrival, wherein several hands of different sizes were passed by in the inside of the cabinet, one of them held a flower which I thought I recognized; but, to be sure, I asked a lady, who sat beside me, what it was. She promptly replied, 'a lily.' I then asked if the hand holding it was meant for me; and it was shown again in token of assent. During my stay, this manifestation was repeated several times; and I have no doubt that the hand with the lily in it was, as it purported to be, my daughter Anna's, and one or more of the smaller hands her sister Mary's. My wife also threw her arms full length, with hands clasped, out of the aperture, on several occasions, always in a night-dress, which I suppose was meant to represent that she wore in her last sickness. The sleeves were uniformly buttoned close to the hand; and I am sure that the exhibition could not have been more natural—including the folds and drapery of the garment—had she made a like manifestation before her departure from earth-life.

"From the first, I had been careful, for obvious reasons, not to mention my wife's or daughter's name. At a seance where there was an attempted demonstration at the aperture, so feeble that I could neither see nor hear distinctly anything that transpired, I was rather startled upon hearing a lady who had but recently arrived, observe, 'She says "Fanny Hagard!"' On asking the lady to repeat the name, she did the first, and said the last sounded something like 'Hagard.' On another occasion, a small star, enveloped in a mist-like halo, passed slowly upward from the bottom of the aperture, and disappeared at the top. This was twice repeated; and, upon my asking that it might show itself again if it was meant to represent my wife, it did so instantly, and remained stationary for a short time before its final disappearance. This was a beautiful manifestation, of which none present could know the full significance but myself. For the last fifteen years my wife has been accustomed to draw a star, through some automatic and writing mediums I sit with, to announce her presence. It appears to be the name she is called by in spirit-life. Often, too, when I sit with trance or clairvoyant mediums, they will say, 'Your star is here.'"

Mary Andrews must feel proud of the foregoing indorsement of her great mediumistic powers. She owes, as do all other advocates of Spiritualism, an immeasurable debt of gratitude to Mr. Hazard for this unbiased account of his visit to Moravia, since the very reputation of the cause largely depends, at present, upon just such intelligent and unprejudiced reports as he has furnished. It is clearly evident that, during my own visit to Moravia, I was, in a measure, inveigled into disbelief by an evil spirit which took advantage of my ignorance of spirit-law and sought to array me on the side of the cold materialistic world; for, even now, I note the presence of an intrepid Diakka, who would persuade me, by means of his oily and venomous spirit-tongue, to doubt even the evidence of Mr. Hazard. This Diakka tells me that he was present at the seances given by Mrs. Andrews, through the entire stay of Mr. Hazard, and that the visitor was completely deluded by the medium in every manifestation.

While I do not directly affirm that any member of the Keeler household, or any visitor, tampered with Mr. Hazard's valise, in search of information, I do say that such an occurrence might easily have taken place—as the valise was unlocked, half the doors in Keeler's house were without locks or bolts, and nearly every room, with the exception of Mrs. Andrews' private apartment, was open most of the time. I furthermore make this broad charge—that all the fraudulent mediums, like Mrs. Andrews, will stoop to almost any trickery when a dollar is at stake, in order to obtain information concerning their victims.

Although Mr. Hazard says, " I said nothing until several days after my arrival at Moravia, in reference to the foregoing spirit-communications," he did unwittingly betray his secret in a hundred different ways, to the medium and others, for eleven days in succession.

The identical Quaker bonnet and cap which the poor deluded man said he had no doubt belonged to his mother, had been recognized by some equally credulous person at nearly every sitting for at least a year previous to Mr. Hazard's visit. Mr. Hazard, who is one of the most credulous of his class, has a sitting with Mrs. Rockwell, who advises him to visit Moravia, when his daughter Anna will hand him a lily, etc. This piece of information Mrs. Rockwell was quite competent to give, not through any mediumistic quality she possessed—for every word uttered by her on that occasion had been unwittingly furnished her by the sitter. Mr. Hazard then proceeds to the residence of Mrs. Staats, and, giving her, directly or indirectly, as he usually does, a full history of his family, and the wonderful sittings he had enjoyed with Mrs. Rockwell and other celebrated mediums, Mrs. Staats was thus enabled, without consulting her spirit-guides, to hand back, in writing, to the gullible old gentleman, the substance of Mrs. Rockwell's communication. These precious documents, together with the two base forgeries purporting to emanate from the spirits of Theodore Parker and Daniel Webster, which are an insult to the common sense as well as the memory of both, the lively spirit-hunter puts into his valise and carries with him to that Mecca of modern Spiritualists, Moravia."

At this point in the Diakka's venomous tirade against the medium, and the glorious cause which she represents, a better spirit appeared and unceremoniously displaced him. This last spirit impressed me with a desire to do Mrs. Andrews the tardy justice of again explicitly stating that *if* there is a genuine materializing spiritual medium in existence, it is Mary Andrews, of Moravia.

CHAPTER IX.

REDEEMING QUALITIES OF THE DIAKKA.

"THE devil is not always so black as he is painted," nor is the Diakka wholly without redeeming qualities. His love for, and devotion to, mediums in adverse circumstances frequently assert themselves in a manner that is marvelous. Many a poor medium can truthfully testify to the kindly assistance of the Diakka in financial matters, by which he has been saved from absolute starvation. The Diakka is also often employed by higher spirits, and renders them efficient service as a detective among the skeptical who are yet in the flesh. Andrew Jackson Davis says, "Under the control, or, rather, by permission of superior minds, the Diakka play important parts in great assaults upon bad governments, upon pernicious organized customs, upon evil social conditions; but for these spiritual freebooters, little progress would be made. The evil communications of the meddlesome mind are, in time, completely overruled for good."

A remarkable instance of the subtle fidelity of the Diakka towards an impecunious medium was once related to me, by such a spirit, through the mouth of that celebrated medium, Joseph Kaffany, as follows:

"Late in the fall of 1879, my medium, Mr. Kaffany, was very poor and much depressed in spirits. His seedy and poverty-stricken appearance rendered him, many times, loth to attend respectable seances, consequently he became an unwilling instrument in our hands. His thin, thread-bare clothing was wholly unfit to protect his person from the storms of approaching winter. In this emergency, I controlled him, and bade him walk boldly into a fashionable clothing-house, where I inspired him with the requisite confidence and judgment to select a comfortable, stylish suit of clothes, which he tried on and found that they fitted to a charm. After making satisfactory arrangements as to the price of the suit, the clerk,—whose salary largely depended upon the gross amount of his sales,—was taken into the confidence of the medium, who directed him to put the goods in a certain peculiar place in the back part of the store, telling him that, within a few hours, some one would call to purchase a suit of this precise character, and that when the garments selected by Kaffany were discovered in a place so unusual, the clerk was to manifest a proper degree of surprise—all of which was faithfully carried out, as the sequel will show. I then persuaded my medium to visit a friendly old soldier, named "Colonel Haskins," who was sojourning at a neighboring hotel. Immediately on our arrival at the Colonel's room, I threw the medium into a dead trance, and, through his unconscious lips, personated the spirit of the great Confucius, saying, "I am Confucius, father of four hundred millions of people. I have come to you, to-night, upon a very important mission. I was selected by the great band of spirits to control this boy who now lies prostrate before you, for the reason that we all know you repose more confidence in me than in all other spirits combined. You know, Colonel, that I would not deceive you; Confucius never stoops to utter falsehood. When in the flesh, my word was law to more than half the population of this globe. I held my great power over the people, by strictly adhering to the truth at all times. Up to the present date, I have never told a lie, either in the physical or the spiritual life, and it is now too late for me to begin. Colonel, look at the form of this poor, pale, poverty-stricken boy! He is suffering for material help, but is too proud to ask for it. We need his services, and, through him, hope, some day, to astonish the world,—but look at his shabby, miserable appearance! In his present condition he is unfit to attend our seances, and we are therefore crippled in our great work. We well know that you are a friend to the cause; that you have spent a great deal of time and money in the investigation and advancement of its glorious truths; that you are a 'simon pure' Spiritualist, as firm as the 'Rock of Ages'; that you do not hang your belief upon the slender thread of evidence alone, but have lashed yourself permanently to the cause by the indestructible cable of faith, which never parts. Those who ridicule such staunch old pioneers in the work as yourself, will find the laugh upon themselves when the light of reason dawns, and science reveals to the world the spiritual knowledge now possessed by the favored few. We have asked favors of you in the past, and have never been refused. It is for this reason that I am here to appeal to your generosity once more. This poor boy through whom I now speak, and who lies in an unconscious condition before you, must be properly clothed, and we ask you to procure the necessary garments for him. It is true that we could materialize the articles ourselves, but our forces are somewhat divided, just now, our *périsprit* is not, as yet, sufficiently attenuated, while many of the best materializers in our band are enjoying a short recreation in the great "Draco Major Belt;" hence it would require vastly greater effort, on our part, to materialize the goods than it would for you to buy them at any clothing-house. Last evening, I came directly through the earth from Hong Kong, at a moment's notice, to attend a great council of our spirit-band, where the matter of clothing this boy was fully discussed. It was finally decided that you should be requested by me, on behalf of the band, to purchase for the boy a good, substantial suit, not alone to aid him and his spirit-guides, but also to make a grand revelation of our power to yourself, as well as, through you, to all your friends.

You must be expeditious, Colonel, as an hour hence I have to attend a spiritual convention on the planet Mars, where I am advertised to personate an Indian chief, who controls a lady speaker. I will hold the boy in dead trance while you go to ———'s Clothing House, call for Mr. ——— and tell him that you wish to look at ——— hold! I will select the clothes myself. I distinctly see a broken suit which will answer every purpose. It will be found in the rear of the store under the last pile of coats on the south tier, among the summer goods. Show the clerk where the garments are, as they have been, for a long time, overlooked. Purchase them, bring them here at once, put them on the boy while he is yet unconscious, and never, in any circumstances, reveal to the medium this delicate secret, as he is a sensitive creature, who would be humiliated almost to distraction by your generosity."

The Colonel did as directed, and, half an hour later, the boy found himself walking in the street neatly attired, and with money in his pocket; and, to this day, Joseph Kaffany, while in his normal condition, will not admit that he knows where or how he secured that very suit of clothes !

Another wonderful instance of the generosity and watchful care of the Diakka over his medium was revealed to me, several years ago, by a jocose spirit, through the physical organism of Joseph Cummings, which I will repeat, as far as possible, in the spirit's own words. He said :

"A band of very select spirits had been working my medium, expressly 'for the good of the cause,' for several months. In their intense desire to make converts, they had too often allowed him to act, under their control, 'without money and without price '—until he was completely broken in health and impoverished in condition. During the temporary absence of the higher control, a consultation was held by a number of trusty Diakka, including myself, when it was resolved that Joe be spirited away from the power of the loftier control for a time, at least until he should recover his health. It was thought advisable to send him to the city of Boston, where he could not only regain his physical soundness, but, during the period of his recreation, would be able to add largely to his spiritual knowledge, by coming in contact with many of the developing mediums for which that city is so justly celebrated. Our meeting was entirely harmonious, every resolution offered was passed without a dissenting vote, and no question worthy of serious consideration arose until the manner of replenishing our medium's exchequer was presented. One Diakka proposed that we order fifty dollars to be materialized at once, and that a committee be appointed to convey the money into the pocket of our medium ; but, before he had finished speaking, half a dozen others simultaneously arose, and, through the jargon that followed, could be heard the voices of various spirits, some proposing to amend the motion by an increase of the amount, while others objected to the whole proceeding as illegal according to spirit law. Soon, however, above the din sounded the gavel of the president, who finally restored order and proceeded to address the meeting as follows :

'Fellow-Diakka : The question before us is one of great magnitude, and needs our most careful consideration. At the least calculation, fifty dollars must be provided to defray the expenses of our dear medium, but how shall it be obtained ? I find, by the new spirit code, that this meeting is not a strictly legal one, owing to the fact that we are not 'in cahoots' with the loftier spirits. Any sort of materialized money would, therefore, be, at best, nothing but a base counterfeit. The exigencies of the case, however, demand immediate and decisive action, and I would be the last one to raise technical points in opposition to this honorable body, were legal obstacles the only ones to be overcome. I find, by a careful examination of the latest official report of the Secretary of the Spirit Treasury, that 'all mints, bullion, and currency, together with all of the dies, plates, and every item of the spiritual machinery, by which money may be materialized, are now within the walls and in the custody of the Grand Royal Spiritual Treasury Department, which lies outside the great 'Draco Major Belt,' through which none of us, in our present condition, are able to pass. If, therefore, there is no objection, I will appoint the spirit before me (referring to myself) who personates Zoroaster, with full power to transfer the requisite amount from the pocket of some mortal who is able to lose it into that of our needy medium, in any manner he may select.' The appointment was fully sustained and the meeting adjourned.

Armed with my new commission, I immediately threw Mr. Cummings into a semi-unconscious state, and, on examining his pockets, found a badly-worn one dollar United States note. I impressed the medium to fold this bill in a peculiar manner so that it could be easily palmed in his left hand, and, instructing him to preserve its folds and hold it fast, induced him to follow me to the home of "Captain Orton," a thorough-bred spiritualist, who reposes great confidence in Zoroaster. Personating that ancient character, I said: 'Captain, you are a great spiritualist and have seen many evidences of life beyond the grave, and, for your fidelity to the cause, we are about to show you a new revelation of spirit power, such as has seldom fallen to the lot of man to witness. Have you a one dollar Government note in your pocket?' The Captain looked anxious and doubtful, but, upon my assurance that Zoroaster would be responsible for his money, took from his pocket a large roll of bills, and, having selected one suitable for the experiment, I requested him to so mark it that it could be afterwards identified. I then caused my medium to fold the bill exactly like the one held in his left hand, and, while the Captain was engaged in recording the number, he slily exchanged them. A moment later, the medium deliberately unfolded the duplicate bill and proceeded to tear it into a thousand pieces. These fragments were then laid upon a plate and, before the eyes of the captain, were deliberately burned to ashes.

The ashes were then placed by the medium in one end of a little magic, or trick, box, while, in the other end of the box, the original bill was dextrously deposited, without arousing the slightest suspicion, on the part of the Captain, that the box contained anything except the ashes of the destroyed note. The box was then placed upon a marble-top centre-table, in full view of the Captain, when Joe began to run around the room, uttering wild and incoherent incantations—then, suddenly stopping, he seized the little box and took from it the identical bill borrowed from the Captain, fully restored. This remarkable exhibition of spirit power in the art of materialization produced the effect of completely mystifying the Captain and of greatly increasing his confidence in Zoroaster. I, therefore, thought it best to strike for the fifty dollar bill while the iron was hot, and proceeded to address him, through the medium, as follows: 'Captain Orton—It has been your good fortune, to-night, to witness one of the most extraordinary evidences of spirit power ever disclosed to man. The de-materialization of money and its full restoration before your very eyes, in the manner just accomplished, is something that may not occur again in the next century. But, marvelous as this experiment appears to you, we have in store one which is infinitely more wonderful. Now, sir, if you will be kind enough to loan me a fifty dollar bill, I will show you a spiritual manifestation that will transcend anything of the kind you have ever seen or dreamed of.' The Captain looked anxious, and seemed reluctant, but, finally, handed over a crisp, new fifty dollar note. This I immediately seized and, tearing off a small corner, handed the fragment to the Captain, requesting him to keep it until the bill should be restored to him—in order to settle, beyond a doubt, the question of its identity. I then read the number and the letter of the bill and, while the Captain was recording them, deftly deposited the currency in a safe place about the person of my medium.

At the same time, I kept rolling his hands, and repeating de-materializing incantations, until the Captain's attention was again attracted, when I opened both the medium's hands, and, to our utter astonishment, the bill had vanished! 'Now, Captain,' I continued, 'I am about to leave you for a short time. You must be patient, and repose full confidence in my integrity. I have shown unbounded confidence in you, by permitting the present exhibition, for few people in earth-life are so highly honored as you have been to-night. In order to complete this last and grandest test, we ask your strict obedience to the following stipulations, under which alone the restoration of your money is possible: Never, in any circumstances, say a word to the medium, or to any living person, in regard to this last manifestation, until the loan is paid. Otherwise you will destroy the conditions relating to the transaction, and render futile every effort on the part of our spirit-band upon which the materialization of your money depends!'

Joe Cummings visited Boston, through our assistance, spent his money freely while it lasted, and made hosts of friends among the developing mediums and other kindred spirits of the Modern Athens; while the Captain remained at home, holding on to the little corner of his fifty dollar note, and anxiously waiting for the spirit of Zoroaster to return and materialize the balance. And he still waits!"

CHAPTER X.

SCIENCE VERSUS SPIRITUALISM.

 VAST amount of unnecessary antagonism exists between many of the so-called scientists and the radical spiritualists, in consequence of the want of more knowledge on the part of each and a better understanding between the two classes. The former frequently charge those who officiate at the spirit-circle with gross unfairness towards the investigator, claiming that the conditions exacted by nearly every medium are such as to preclude a thorough examination, or a strictly scientific analysis, of the phenomena produced; while the latter charge the scientists with bigotry and intolerance, claiming that they have not the moral courage to examine without prejudice, and impartially to

report upon, spiritual manifestations, as they do upon other subjects, from the fear of making themselves unpopular with the masses, or that the result of an honest inquiry may demolish some old established theory or belief. But nothing can be farther from the truth than these extreme views of either class.

The truly conservative spiritualists of to-day have no fear of investigation, but heartily welcome the most searching inquisitions of every candid scientist, no matter how firmly he may be intrenched in his materialistic opinions. They court a thorough study of all spirit phenomena, from all quarters, and seek for light in every direction where they have reason to hope it may be found. They believe that the scientist, when fully conversant with the laws that govern spirit phenomena, and the methods by which they are produced, will be an advantage to the cause, for *Science is really the friend and not the enemy of Spiritualism, since truth must eventually be triumphant.*

It is only the illiterate, the new-fledged,

half-converted, semi-orthodox, "crank" of a spiritualist, who opposes scientific research. It is this class which hangs its dead weight upon the cause of Spiritualism, clogging the wheels of progress by continually demanding of the spirits apparent impossibilities, thereby shutting out of the spirit-circle hosts of honest investigators.

Nearly every denomination in the religious world has had this same class of ignorant fanatics to contend with. Christianity has, for centuries, been freighted down, almost to the water's edge, by these ignorant and indiscreet adherents. It was this same class of possibly honest, but, certainly, ignorant and unbalanced people who held up their hands in holy horror when the scientists first began to demonstrate to the world the great antiquity of this earth. These persons, laboring under the fanatical delusion that they were obliged to defend and preserve to everlasting a fixed religious opinion, right or wrong, said to the great geologists and astronomers, "The God we worship, created this world six thousand years ago. He completed the work in six literal days, 'And on the seventh day God ended his work which he had made; and he rested on the seventh day from all his work which he had made.' These days were evidently composed of twenty-four hours each, 'for the evening and the morning were the first day,' and so on to the seventh day, when God ended his work and rested. When you attempt to distort six thousand years into as many millions, or, by your superior scholarship, to prove that the six days of creation were six vast, indefinite periods of time, you belie our divinely-inspired record, which plainly designates each day by 'the evening and the morning;' you mock our religion, which is founded upon and almost wholly sustained by the revelations of these sacred records; you belittle the works of the Deity by trying to distort the supernatural into the natural. You are a wicked, dangerous class of men, who ought to be suppressed, with all your counterfeit science and damnable philosophy."

But the true scientists, who are not cowards, but honest, intrepid men, quietly and laboriously pursued their investigations, diving down deep into the earth, regardless of consequences—preferring to read the history of creation in God's own hand-writing, which He has plainly traced on every rock and every strata of the earth's formation.

At last, after ages of useless and cruel opposition, after millions of valuable lives have been sacrificed, after whole nations have been destroyed and countless treasures wasted in the vain hope to check the march of science, these misguided zealots awoke to the fact—plainly demonstrated by scientific research—that, after all, a little difference in time need not necessarily dethrone their Deity or destroy their religion; that it does not detract, in the least, from the power of the Creator if He chose to take more than six days in which to fashion this grand old earth of ours.

Additional age does not detract from the quality of this globe, but rather serves to continually improve it. There was a time when many of these same good, honest people believed that man was created upon a certain day, and that, out of a rib taken from his side, a woman was constructed. And when the idea was advanced, by some scientists, that man was older than six thousand years, and that it required vastly more than that length of time, after the appearance of this planet, to render it fit for human habitation—that man has been coming up from the lower order of animal life, for millions of years, and that his creation began countless ages ago, away down among the trilobites, these simple-minded people were absolutely horrified, and thought to lose their religion, and the Creator they worship, through the advancement and propagation of such monstrous ideas. But the men of science kept quietly at work, in search of truth wherever it was likely to be found, replying to these mistaken zealots, "We do not wish to interfere with your religion, or to disparage or dismiss your Deity. We are only in search of facts.

If we fail to credit God with the miraculous creation of the first two human beings exactly in accordance with the inspired account, we do Him vastly greater honor when we prove, by consulting His works, the broad fact that there was a time when this earth was a red-hot ball of fire, and that no man lived, or could have lived, upon it—while, to-day, we trace to His creative power the existence of over thirteen hundred millions of human beings. Shall it be said that a fact so grand as this depreciates His immeasurable power or dims His ineffable glory?"

CHAPTER IX.

THE GREAT MATERIALIZED STONE.

DURING the winter of 1876-77, spiritual circles were regularly held at the house of Dr. S. C. Jasebrow, in the City of Syracuse. These circles were attended by a large number of persons, most of whom became very much interested in the phenomena which occurred. After the spirit-band which controlled the circle became well organized and disciplined, they promised to give, at a subsequent meeting, a remarkable demonstration of their power, in the materialization of some keepsake for the family. Every possible arrangement was made, by strictly obeying the injunctions of the spirits, to render the trial a success. At the appointed time, more than the usual number were present, including several bankers, two reporters for local papers, one military officer and other prominent citizens. More than ordinary caution was observed in closing the doors and windows of the spirit-room, before the circle was formed, so that every member of the company might be satisfied that all means of both ingress and egress had been effectually cut off. We sat around a common dining-table, so close to each other that our chairs nearly touched. After joining hands upon the table, to complete the circle, and make sure that no person could break into or leave it, the lights were extinguished. Half an hour, or more, had passed without any manifestation, when there appeared, directly over the center of the table, two tiny lights, which were plainly visible to every person in the room. These appearances gradually approached each other, until they merged into one, which seemed to be about the size of a man's head. A moment later, there was a terrible crash which shook the whole house. When the lights were restored, the circle was found unbroken, and the doors and windows still closed and locked; but, on the table, was discovered a huge singularly-shaped rock, weighing upwards of eighty pounds. So great was the force of its fall that two slates lying upon the table, at the time, were broken into a hundred fragments, some of which were driven more than half an inch into the hard oak table. Consternation was depicted upon every countenance. Never was there a more convincing test of spirit power in the line of materialization. Here was a huge boulder created by the spirits before our very eyes, under such conditions as apparently precluded the possibility of collusion or fraud. Next day, the local papers were teeming with accounts of the mystery, which were copied by the press generally. No one could be found who would acknowledge that he could trace the origin of the stone, or knew to what family of rock it belonged. One competent geologist ventured to say that it slightly resembled a meteoric stone. Dr. John F. Boynton, the eminent scientist, who has lec-

MATERIALIZED STONE.

tured to crowded houses in nearly every city of the Union, called, by particular request, and examined the stone very minutely, but could not be prevailed upon to express any opinion as to its precise geological character. And still the mystery remained unsolved!

A few weeks later, by special direction of the spirit band, quite a large number of persons again assembled at the house of Doctor Jasebrow to make inquiry as to the manner in which the stone was created. While one of the members of the circle was giving his opinion, he suddenly lost consciousness, and the spirit of Carl Augustus Muhlenburg took possession of his form, through it addressing the audience as follows:

"My friends: It is with extreme difficulty that I am enabled to control the material instrument through which I now speak. If I can succeed, however, in holding him in a dormant condition long enough to accomplish my purpose, I will try, partially at least, to explain the manner in which our spirit-band succeeded in accomplishing the herculean task of manufacturing, from the invisible elements, this ponderous mineral substance. As there are persons comprised in your circle to-night, who may never before have witnessed what I am now exhibiting through this instrumentality, *i. e.* 'dead control,' I will first endeavor to make you acquainted with this particular phase of spirit phenomena. Understand that Mr. T., whose physical body I am temporarily occupying, is utterly dead to all that surrounds him. While his intelligence is not completely divorced from the physical casket, he is, for the time being, utterly oblivious to any existence at all. He is, therefore, more truly dead to what is now transpiring than if he had actually vacated the flesh forever. Had he passed away, and left the form entirely, breaking the last link that binds the spiritual to the material body, he would, at once, take on new spiritual senses, in place of his physical ones, and thus could understand all that is now taking place, even more readily and clearly than any of my hearers. But, in his present condition, called, as I have intimated, dead control, his intellectual faculties are numb and dormant, completely paralysed by coming within the radius of my *périspirit*. The heart beats naturally, only its motion is slightly accelerated; the blood circulates freely; respiration, and the other operations of the body necessary to sustain life, proceed as if nothing unusual had happened. In this condition, he falls an easy victim to spirit power. I enter his physical structure and am now using it at my will. Note how easily I control every muscle and every portion of his body. His tympanum arrests the undulations of sound, and carries the vibrations to the brain for my benefit, *but not for record*. His physical eye sees, in the same manner, for the benefit of the temporary occupant only. No record can be made upon his brain, since its custodian and scribe lies powerless under my *périspirit*. The sense of feeling belongs to the same category. If you should thrust a pin into the flesh of this instrument, I alone would feel the pain. Observe with what ease I handle this physical form. See how I raise these arms, and open these hands and gesticulate with them, as if they were my very own. Notice me while I open his watch, and, with his eyes, ascertain the time. So perfect and natural are all our movements through dead control, that I am not surprised when I hear some skeptical people, in the form, who cannot comprehend the grand idea of the transmigration of souls, declare that they do not believe either in spirits or Pythagoras. But I have wandered from my subject—let us return to the great mystery of the Stone.

Understand, my friends, I labor under great disadvantage in attempting to explain this materializing phenomena to you, from the fact that I can only communicate with you through the medium of your grosser physical senses. Had any member of this circle been born blind, so that his physical eye had never felt the light, imagine, for a moment, how utterly impossible it would be for him to comprehend the beauties of a landscape. Now, every one of you—with the exception of those who are clairvoyant or clairaudient—are deaf and blind to every spiritual sense which we recognise, and through which we obtain information; therefore, I am compelled to stop, condense, dilute and translate, as I go along, in order to bring my language within the scope of your circumscribed comprehension. This earth, by the action of wind, rain, snow and the sun's rays, is constantly throwing off vast amounts of vaporous and gaseous properties, which are generated by the decomposition of animal and vegetable matter. These gases, which, when condensed by means of our wonderful appliances, yield solid and substantial matter, are, when thrown off, so rarefied as to be lighter than the air you breathe ; consequently they readily ascend to the upper belt of atmosphere, where all the watery portion, together with nearly all of the balance, is condensed, and returned to the earth in the form of rain or snow. There is, however, a continual loss during these transformations. Some of the rarer gases, unaffected by variations in temperature, continue to pass on, undergoing a definite chemical change at a point about ten miles from the earth's surface, which makes them still more volatile. Thus they continue in their upward journey, until they are so remote as to become wholly independent of the influence of the earth's attraction. Here, these gases undergo still another change, and begin slowly to condense. Vast belts of this ethereal substance now revolve, after the fashion of asteroids and planetoids, imitating, upon a small scale, the nebular process of world-making, until a red-hot mass of solid matter—a miniature earth—is formed, which continues to revolve on its axis, and to fly through space until it comes within reach of the earth's attraction, or that of some other and larger solid body, by which it is promptly absorbed, just as a meteoric stone falls to the earth. In constructing the stone which lies before you, we were not obliged to go through the long and tedious process of creating a miniature asteroid. Still, the nebular system just described will furnish you with the key to our process. The material of which this stone is composed, we found, in vast quantities, hovering over the large manufacturing establishments of your city. As soon as the design of our band was made known to the spiritual world, through a system very similar to your telegraph and telephone, a million willing spirit-hands quickly brought an abundance of the crude matter, which was reduced, by rapid condensation, to the lowest possible point of gaseous materialization. Through the open doors and windows of this house, defying your imperfect physical vision, this, to you, invisible matter was brought into the circle-room, before the lights were extinguished. We immediately summoned one hundred thousand expert chemists from our Royal Æsthetical Laboratory of Spiritual Science, and, through a process which I cannot describe so that you will be able to comprehend it by means of your inadequate physical senses, we, Gorgon-like, accomplished the complete condensation of these gases at the point where the greater light appeared, namely, just twenty inches directly over the centre of the table. The moment the gases reached this point of condensation, they became too gross to further resist the indomitable power of gravitation, and the stone fell, crushing to atoms the two slates and driving, by its ponderous weight, many fragments deep into the bed of the table. But I am growing weak in my control of this medium, and will now leave him, so quietly that he will never know, unless actually informed, that he has been in a dormant condition and has constituted my temporary mouth-piece and interpreter. You will observe that, the moment I leave the casket, and Mr. T. returns to a normal condition, he will resume the conversation exactly at the point where it was interrupted."

The ubiquitous Diakka, ever on the alert

to obtain a foothold in every well-organized and successful spirit-band, utterly failed to interpose sufficient force, at the time the stone was created, to prevent, or even to retard, the experiment. Jealous and envious of the spirits' great success in the present instance, he indignantly retired, vowing eternal vengeance and declaring that he would, at no distant day, capture and influence some member of this very circle, employ his powers in exposing the trick, and prove the whole transaction a fraud and a delusion. Accordingly, a few months later, he inclosed in his toils Mr. Joseph Cafferty, a member of Doctor Jasebrow's household, and one of the principal mediums through which the phenomenon of the Stone was accomplished. Under the influence of this most desperate of all spiritual beings, Mr. Cafferty subsequently gave to some of his confreres the following easy explanation of this seemingly wonderful occurrence:

"After Muhlenburg and myself had promised to perform some great act in spiritual jugglery, transcending all previous efforts in the same direction, I found myself constantly studying by what means I might devise something novel, startling and conclusive. One day, while riding in a carriage with Mr. T., another member of the circle, whose spirit-control is often in collusion with my spirit-guides, we visited the works of the Syracuse Water Company, at a point where a new reservoir was in progress of construction. A very deep excavation had been made at the north end of the embankment, passing through a gravelly ravine, evidently produced by an ancient water-course. Out of the bottom of this deep cut, the workmen had thrown a large number of smooth, round stones. My attention was particularly attracted to one, weighing about eighty pounds, which seemed different from anything of the stone kind which I had ever seen. A voice whispered within me,—I being a clairaudient, heard it distinctly,—saying, 'That's a good job to put up on the great magnetic healer, Doctor Jasebrow.' Quick as thought, I bounded out of the carriage, seized the stone, and deposited it safely beneath the seat. Imagine my surprise, when I spoke to my companion, to find him in a deep trance, entirely oblivious to all that had occurred. We drove home, and, as my companion did not mention the circumstance, I said nothing concerning it to him. That evening, under direction of the spirits in control, I repaired to his carriage-house and, in a common grain-bag, removed the stone to a place of safety. On the evening preceding that upon which the stone made its appearance, I was out late, and found, upon my return home, that the family had all retired. An inspiration seized me to the effect that this would be a good opportunity to bring in the stone from the garden, where it had been concealed in order to have it in readiness to assist the spirits on the following evening. I did so, and, under the direction of my guides, concealed the stone in an old trunk, at the foot of the bed in my own dormitory, which is contiguous to the circle-room. At an early hour, on the following evening, while the guests were assembling, still urged by my spirit-guides, I put the stone in an old flag-bottomed chair. There was a break in the flags, sufficient to allow the stone to sink down nearly half way out of sight. As it was warm, I took off my coat and carelessly threw it over the back of the chair, but in such a manner that it hung down over the seat, completely concealing the stone. After arranging the circle, and the lights had been slightly dimmed, I brought out my chair, stone and all. Seating myself next to, and at the right of, an individual whose guide was a confederate of the spirit influencing me, I passed his hand over to an old gentleman who was seated at my right. In this manner the circle was completed. All hands were joined except my own, which were free. It was as dark as Egypt, and, as there was no noise to cover my movements, I remained perfectly quiet for a quarter of an hour or more. At last, some one struck up the song of 'John Brown's body lies mouldering in the grave,' and the whole company joined in the chorus. By this time, the spirits had generated enough power, together with sufficient *périsprit*, for their use, and I heard my spirit-guides whisper, ' Go on, Joe!' I immediately took from my pocket a small phial containing almond oil and phosphorus, and, covering it with a thick handkerchief, raised the ground-glass stopper a trifle, and, when the oxygen of the air entered the bottle, the contents blazed up so vividly that I feared the light would disclose me to the circle. But the spirits, as usual, were equal to the emergency, and, at once, instructed me to press the stopper down tight—when the light slowly vanished. I then took the brimstone end of a match between the moist thumb and forefinger of each hand, and, extending my arms to the utmost, over the table, opened and shut the fingers rapidly, the matches, each time, giving off a beautiful, tiny, phosphorescent light. I now deliberately brought both hands together, and created the great light by means of the bottle of phosphorus, and, when the light had vanished, returned the bottle to my pocket. Then, seizing the stone, I raised it, as high as I could reach, over the table, and let it fall directly upon the slates.

"Of course, there was a great crash and much commotion ; and, during the excitement, the spirits took proper care of me. When the lights were restored, the circle was found to be unbroken. And these are the 'BOTTOM FACTS' in the history of the Great Materialized Stone."

CHAPTER XII.

SEANCES WITH CHARLES H. FOSTER.

DURING the year 1872, I visited the celebrated ballot-test medium, Charles H. Foster, at his home in New York City. At the first sitting, I wrote, as requested by the medium, on slips of paper prepared by himself, the names of several of my deceased acquaintances, and so folding them that the contents would be unknown to any one except myself, placed them together on the center of the table and awaited the result. In a moment, Mr. Foster took the whole bundle of ballots in his left hand, and, passing them rapidly across his forehead, one at a time, dropped upon the table what I supposed to be the same ballots. A moment after, he remarked, "My impressions sometimes come slowly," and, handing me a card upon which the alphabet was printed, asked me to read off the letters, when he hesitatingly spelled out one of the names I had written. Several other names were then correctly given, when he again raised the whole of the ballots to his forehead, and, suddenly dropping them, pointed to one, saying, "That person is Julia King, your mother." I replied, "The name is correct, but the relationship is wrongly stated." Handing me another ballot, he said, "Your mother's name is Sarah Johnson." Again I said, "The relationship you mention does not exist, although I did write the name you give, which is that of a friend in spirit-life."

At the request of Mr. Foster, I asked my spirit-friends if any of them could communicate with me, when three raps were distinctly heard, which indicated that they could. I then asked if any one of them could tell me my own name. Mr. Foster replied, "As the spirits you desire to communicate with are not as yet in full *rapport* with me, their influence being very weak, you will be obliged to write upon a card three names, including your own, when the spirts will endeavor to assist me in selecting your name." By this time I began to be suspicious that the only spirits present were my own and that of Charles H. Foster. I, however, took the card and wrote, in rather a poor hand, my own name first; the name Henry Stillwell was then written in a little better style, but the last name, Samuel Johnson, I dashed off in an easy, flowing manner, making it look more like the signature of a business man than either of the others. Mr. Foster then took the card, and, under the guidance of his spirit-band, guessed the names in exact reverse of the order in which I had written them—thus selecting my own name last. I paid Mr. Foster five dollars for the sitting and promised to call again the next day, when, he assured me, the power would be stronger, and, consequently, the manifestations much more satisfactory.

On relating my experience to a friend, and

declaring my suspicions that Foster cheated me, by dexterously throwing upon the table a bundle of duplicate ballots, while he slily read the originals, my friend was very anxious to accompany me on the following day, and, if possible, assist in solving the mystery. Accordingly, he prepared three slips of bright red paper, upon which he wrote the names of three deceased persons. Upon our arrival at the rooms of the great medium, we found him in good spirits. He greeted me by my own name, and seemed well pleased because I had brought a friend with me. The spirits were very communicative; they could give me the name of the hotel where I stopped, as well as that of the play which I had witnessed on the previous evening, together with much other trivial and common-place information, already in my possession. But to the contents of the red slips of paper prepared by my friend, neither Mr. Foster nor any of his spirit-band could give the slightest clue. Again, I contributed five dollars to the great medium's exchequer, for a half-hour's sitting, and retired from his august presence a "sadder, but a wiser man." Both myself and my friend were satisfied that he had cheated me, and that, by some legerdemain, he had read all the ballots upon which I had written; but just how he accomplished the adroit feat, while our eyes were fastened upon him, we were at a loss to divine.

This mystery furnished me with ample food for thought during the several months which intervened between my second and third sitting. I had noticed, at each interview, that Mr. Foster, who is an inveterate smoker, had a great deal of trouble to keep his cigar alight. Half a dozen times, during each sitting, he would strike a match, and, holding it in a peculiar manner, as if he was in the open air, where a strong wind was blowing, would take a whiff or two, and then allow the cigar to go out again. After carefully comparing notes with several reliable persons who had held seances with the same medium, I came to the conclusion, deduced from their experience as well as my own, that Mr. Foster invariably changed the ballots, and that, while the duplicate blanks lay upon the table before his victims, and he was engaged in the troublesome task of relighting his cigar, he was, at the same time, reading, by the aid of the very match so carelessly employed, an open ballot held in the palm of his right hand. Armed with this hypothesis, I again visited this celebrated medium, some six months subsequent to my second interview.

It was evident, from Mr. Foster's manner, that he had entirely forgotten me, and I did not acquaint him with the fact that we had ever met before.

We sat down at a table, in the usual manner, and the medium handed me six small pieces of tissue-paper, upon each of which, at his request, I wrote the name of a deceased friend. I then rolled each slip into a pellet and placed them together on the center of the table. Mr. Foster took them into his hand, and, after muttering some unintelligible words, returned what seemed to be the identical pellets to the table. Again was I requested to point out the letters of the alphabet, from a card, upon which they were printed, and, while thus engaged, I noticed that the medium experienced fresh trouble in lighting his cigar. After several matches had been destroyed in this apparently fruitless attempt, Mr. Foster picked up one of the little paper balls, and slowly spelled out one of the names I had written, and, pointing it out, requested me to see if the spirits were correct. I did so, and, at the same time, seized the other five pellets, which proved, upon examination, to be *every one of them a blank!* So quickly did I accomplish this little piece of strategy that the medium scarcely realized his dilemma before it was too late to successfully meet it. In a moment, Foster was in a towering rage. He ordered me out of his house, swore that he would call the police, and demanded his pay for the sitting, all in the same breath. I took it all very coolly, for I had met such mountebanks before, and knew that, as a rule, " Barking dogs seldom bite." After his obstreperous wrath had somewhat subsided, I quietly said, " Mr. Foster, is your malady owing to mental trouble, or are you suffering from the attack of a remorseless Diakka?" He looked at me, for a moment, in amazement, when I smiled and it was not long before we both broke into a hearty laugh. I told him that he was one of the best actors I had ever met, and he returned the compliment by telling me a fact, which I had never before suspected, that I was a medium of no small calibre.

Foster then explained to me many hitherto inexplicable mysteries. He said that I had been permitted to discover a clue to the methods, by which the spirits put themselves *en rapport* with him, owing to the fact that I had arrived at such an advanced state in my investigations that the spirits were convinced they could begin to trust me with their secrets. He congratulated me upon my development in spiritual knowledge thus far; and declared that he could plainly foresee bright prospects before me, as a medium, in the near future.

He would caution me against confiding the secrets of the spirit-world to any who are unable to bear them. "The time may come," he continued, "when this world will be developed to such a state of spiritual perfection that it will answer to reveal the true science of spiritual phenomena, but, to-day, and for many years to come, our secrets must be carefully confined to the chosen few. In our present crude state of development, the ordinary investigator of spirit phenomena is in nowise to be trusted. In this case, as in many others, confidence must be a plant of slow growth."

Ten years have elapsed since Charles H. Foster uttered the foregoing sentiments, every word of which my after experience fully corroborates. To have turned, at that moment, the science of spiritual communion loose among the masses, would have destroyed the system altogether; but, to-day, the world is better prepared for spiritual truth, and accepts evidence rather for its quality than its quantity.

There may be, however, isolated cases, even

in this enlightened age, where the conditions exacted in the spirit-circle, will shut out the full sunlight of truth from the most conscientious investigator, but such cases are now wholly unworthy of serious consideration, for "truth is mighty and will prevail."

Fig. H
Spirits getting *en-rapporte* through the BALLOT TEST.

CHAPTER XIII.

INTERVIEWS WITH DOCTOR HENRY SLADE.

THE day following my third interview with Charles H. Foster, I called upon that famous slate-writer, Doctor Henry Slade, of New York city, whose reputation as a physical and mental test-medium stands second to none. Upon entering his apartments, I was received by his assistant, who inquired my name and the nature of my business. I gave him the required information, when he requested me to be seated until Mr. Slade should be disengaged. I was not obliged to wait long before the great medium made his appearance, when we at once proceeded to business. We seated ourselves at a common, old-fashioned dining-table, with leaves extended. Mr. Slade sat at my left, with the corner of the table projecting between us. I had hardly assumed the sitting posture, when a vacant chair, on the opposite side of the table, moved several inches toward me. A picture upon the side wall vibrated quite perceptibly, and without any visible cause. The Doctor appeared very nervous, and, grasping my hands in his own, told me that he was afraid of the spirits—that I must hold on to him for protection, and must, in no circumstances, break the circle, or the spirits might injure us both. In a few moments, I distinctly felt something touching me and pulling at my clothing, as if there was some one under the table. Directly, something came up into my lap, which Mr. Slade said was a materialized spirit-hand trying to reach my neck-tie. I was not in a good position to use my eyes, as the Doctor held me very close to the table, although I did get a glimpse of something in my lap that looked not so much like a hand as a human foot. Suspecting —in my ignorance of spiritual laws—that the Doctor himself was the direct author of that particular phase of the phenomenon, I affected to be alarmed, which appeared to please Slade excessively. Watching my opportunity, when the "spirit-hand" was playing its most venturesome tricks, I suddenly recoiled from the table, apparently horror-stricken, just in time to detect the Doctor in the act of withdrawing from my lap his left foot, which he quickly replaced in his slipper. As my appearance did not indicate anything but terror, and an irresistible impulse to remove myself from the influence of the capricious spirits, the Doctor little suspected that I had discovered the means by which they had produced the phenomenon. He then told me, that I was a very mediumistic individual, and altogether too sensitive, in my crude, undeveloped condition, to endure materializing exhibitions of so high an order. After being assured by him that there was no danger to be apprehended from the spirits, through their efforts, at slate-writing, I consented to sit with him once more. The Doctor then took up a common slate, and, after carefully cleaning both sides, placed it under the leaf of the table, holding it with his right hand, in such a manner that the slate was wholly hidden from my view while only the thumb of his right hand, with which he grasped the table leaf, was visible. At the medium's request, I took hold of the opposite end of the slate with my left hand, and joined my right with the Doctor's left, upon the centre of the table. A crumb of pencil had been placed upon the upper side of the slate before it disappeared from our vision. In this position we waited several minutes, when the sound of writing was distinctly heard. I could plainly see the movements of the cords in the Doctor's wrist, indicating to me that *he* was doing the writing, but I was not sure of this fact, at the time, as he appeared to be very nervous, making many strange and, apparently, unnecessary movements. When the writing ceased, the slate was quickly jerked out of our hands, by some invisible agency, and, during the Doctor's effort to regain it, I was quite sure that it was turned completely over. On withdrawing the slate, a short message of trivial import, which I cannot now recall—except the closing words, " Come again, Allie "—appeared upon the upper surface. The Doctor then cleaned the slate, preparatory to another experiment, when a loud rap sounded upon the door, which the medium answered in person, carelessly taking the slate with him. While he engaged in a low conversation with some one at the door, the slate was hidden from my view only for a few seconds, but, during that brief period, I had a deep impression (which I have since been told was a Diakka influence), that the interruption was pre-arranged with his assistant in order to give Slade an opportunity to exchange the clean slate for one that had been written upon. The Doctor then returned to the table, and, laying the slate down upon it, a little beyond my reach, without exhibiting its under side, we resumed our former positions at the table, he holding both my hands in such a manner that neither of us could be accused of being instrumental in producing the phenomenon. In a very few moments, the scratching of a slate-pencil, which I could not definitely locate, was distinctly heard. The noise continued for several minutes, and, when it ceased, a long, well-written communication, addressed to myself, signed " Henry Truesdell," was found upon the under side of the slate. As the message contained no information of special importance to me—the writer being a myth—I did not care to preserve it. I then frankly told Mr. Slade that the sitting had been quite unsatisfactory—the physical part being very bunglingly executed, while the communications purporting to be written by the spirits, since they actually proceeded from entire strangers, were to me vague and meaningless. The Doctor expressed great surprise at my dissatisfaction, saying that, from a physical point of view, the manifestations I had witnessed could not be excelled in

Fig. 8.

a score of sittings. The communications, he admitted, were not quite so convincing as he had hoped for, a fact which he explained upon the hypothesis that I was too much alarmed to allow the safe appearance of my immediate spirit-friends, and that strangers had, therefore, been substituted to prepare the way. He assured me that the road was now clear, so that, at any future sitting, my spirit-friends would be able to identify themselves, and to communicate with me more freely. I then promised to obey " Allie's " injunction to come again. Parting with a five-dollar note, which I thought would fully compensate the Doctor for an hour's sitting, I bade him good bye, feeling a trifle poorer in filthy lucre, but inestimably richer in spiritual knowledge.

A few months after my first interview with Doctor Slade, I had occasion to repeat my visit to New York, when I again called upon this noted medium. I was ushered into his spacious drawing-room by the same attendant who received me on the former occasion, who made the usual inquiries regarding my name and the nature of my business. I told him the object of my visit, but begged to be excused from divulging my identity at present, saying that the manifestations, should any occur, would be much more satisfactory to me if I could be allowed to remain *incognito* for a time — at least until the spirits themselves should disclose my name. Not wishing to assist the spirits in identifying me, in case the medium should not, I took the precaution, before my arrival, to remove my name from the lining of my hat, but intentionally left in my overcoat pocket an unsealed letter which would convey to the physical eye the erroneous impression that my name was Samuel Johnson, of Rome, N. Y. The attendant at once took charge of my outer garment and left me alone in the spirit-room to await the coming of the renowned Doctor. Incited by curiosity, I began to look about me, examining every part of the room in a thorough and critical manner. There was, in the apartment, a piece of furniture, resembling a large sideboard, which rested upon legs but a few inches in length. Under this article of furniture I discovered a common slate, upon the lower surface of which there appeared a communication in substance as follows:

"We are happy to meet you in this atmosphere of spiritual research. You are now surrounded by many anxious friends in spirit-life who desire to communicate with you, but cannot, until you learn more of the laws which govern their actions. If you will come here often, your spirit-friends will soon be able to identify themselves and to communicate with you as in earth-life. ALLIE."

Inspired by what I have since become convinced was a Diakka influence, I had a strong impression that this was one of the Doctor's stereotyped messages, suitable for almost any occasion, and intended for the next gudgeon who might stray into his net. I therefore wrote under "Allie's" communication, in a bold hand, as follows:

"Henry! look out for this fellow—he is up to snuff! ALCINDA."*

I immediately replaced the slate in its original position, and seated myself in another part of the room. A few moments later, the great connecting-link between our world and the next—known to mortals as Slade—entered the room. I saw, at once, that he did not remember having met me before; so I apologized for not giving my name, saying that I would prefer to have the spirits ferret it out. The Doctor was in good humor, and at once promised to do all in his power to aid me in the line of spirit investigation. We sat in the usual manner, at a table situated nearly in the center of the room, around which the Doctor had previously placed several chairs. In these, he claimed, the spirits of deceased friends were accustomed to sit. We had scarcely joined hands, when some of the empty chairs began to move, impelled, I concluded, by the spirits,

* Alcinda was the name of Doctor Slade's deceased wife, of which fact I was cognizant.

through the agency of the medium's long, lithe legs and bare feet, which fact I seemed to detect in his countenance and the contortions of his visible body. After these physical manifestations were concluded, the Doctor brought in, from the adjoining room, a slate, which was the exact duplicate of the one I had seen lying beneath the sideboard, and, placing it under the leaf of the table, we both held it for the spirits to write upon. Directly a scratching noise was heard, apparently emanating from the slate. After the sound had ceased, the slate was withdrawn and inspected, when the name " Mary Johnson " appeared plainly written upon it. I pretended to be a little startled at this manifestation, and probably looked quite serious for the moment ; but, when the medium told me that Mary Johnson was my sister, I felt in duty bound to correct him, since no such person has any right to claim relationship with me. Not in the least disconcerted by this trivial error on the part of the spirits, the Doctor, under the pretext of changing the light, drew the table very near to the sideboard where the great slate-bait had been concealed by the Diakka. We were again seated at the table, in nearly the same positions already described in the account of my first interview with the Doctor. The magnetism was so strong, and the spirits were so active, that we partially lost control of the slate, and it fell to the floor. Keeping our positions as well as we could, in the circumstances, the Doctor reached down his right hand to regain possession of the slate, but the indomitable Diakka was too quick for him, and caused him, instead of grasping the slate that fell, to bring up the duplicate. Several ineffectual attempts were then made to obtain writing under the table-leaf, when it was decided that the force was too strong, and the Doctor placed the slate on the center of the table, with the clean side uppermost. He then put some fragments of slate-pencil beneath it, and we again joined hands. A moment after, the table began to tremble violently, and Slade appeared much agitated, when we distinctly heard the spirits writing upon the slate. The sound was unmistakable; even the crossing of the t's and the dotting of the i's could be easily distinguished. This was the grandest victory of my life! Inaudibly I exclaimed, "Eureka! Eureka!" After years of fruitless search for proof of the immortality of man, at last I had found it. There we were, face to face, as it were, with our spirit-friends, communicating with them as in earth-life, with the unimpeachable testimony of our eyes and ears to establish the fact! At the conclusion of the writing, the Doctor raised the slate and turned it over in a triumphant manner, when his eyes fell upon the *two* messages. He seemed appalled! Had a thunderbolt from heaven fallen at his feet, he could not have been more astounded. For several minutes he continued to gaze upon the slate in blank amazement—then, suddenly turning upon me, his countenance livid with rage and excitement, he exclaimed, "What does this mean? Who has been meddling with this slate?" "Spirits," I coolly replied. A moment later, this great manipulator of unseen forces was as mellow as a ripe apple. Freely and fully we communed together for an hour or more, upon the all-important subject of my visit. If I had heretofore been suspicious of the Doctor, now every shadow of doubt was dispelled. The science of Spiritualism was more thoroughly discussed between us than I had ever before heard it, the Doctor taking especial pains to explain to me many of the mysterious methods adopted by the spirits, in order to reach those who are yet in the physical form. I was thus highly favored, the Doctor informed me, for the reason that the spirits desired more fully to develop my wonderful mediumistic powers. "It is seldom," he continued, "that we can find a person fit to be trusted with the great secrets of our wonderful and delicate spirit-manifestations, but, from you, we are ready to acknowledge, we have nothing more to conceal. You are now qualified to enjoy all the spiritual knowledge that is attainable by mortals. We cheerfully welcome you to our royal ranks as a true and absolute medium, through whom we hope to make many converts to our glorious cause."

I left the metropolis and returned to my home, pondering upon the spiritual lessons I had learned. A new light from the spirit-world now dawned upon me. After fifteen years of almost fruitless search for spiritual knowledge, I now, for the first time, began to realize that I had been seeking it in contrary directions and through wrong methods. I had, by my skeptical and unyielding opposition, repeatedly driven away the good spirits and encouraged the Diakka in their mischief, when I should have reversed this order of things. I had laid snares and traps for many a poor medium, and thus impeded his progress, when I should have given him my confidence and support. But, now, all was changed. A new feeling came over me—one of intense joy, mingled with not a little pride; for I had just learned the all-important fact, that Spiritualism is not only a science but an Art. I was no longer a novice, a mere investigator, but a teacher—a full-fledged medium, bearing with me the verbal endorsement of the two greatest spirit-manipulators in all the world.

Quietly I began to experiment at my home, giving private circles to my friends only; but it was not possible that such light could long remain concealed under a bushel. Crowds of curious people, embracing almost every class in society, came pouring in upon me, until, for self-protection, I was obliged to discontinue my sittings, for a time, announcing to all inquirers that the reported manifestations had but little foundation in fact. But the seed had been sown, and there was no avoiding the harvest. The news spread like wild-fire, among the faithful, that I had been converted to the cause, and hundreds of spiritualists, from all quarters, sent me their hearty congratulations; so rapidly did I rise in the spiritual ranks, so astounding and miraculous were the reported phenomena occurring through my influences, that, within four months after my ordination by Slade and Foster, I even began myself to doubt my suddenly-acquired gifts. This delusion was only dispelled after I had held sittings with professional mediums, clairvoyants, clairaudients and spirit-healers, by the score, who claimed to have discovered my control and to clearly recognize my spirit-guides.

CHAPTER XIV.

ONE OF MY MAIDEN SITTINGS.

AMONG the first of my amateur sittings reported for the press was the one referred to in the following article, written by the late Daniel J. Halstead, then proprietor of the *Syracuse Daily Courier:*

"Thinking that a little something besides politics might be acceptable these days, and having an opportunity, last Saturday evening, by invitation, to witness a seance at a friend's house in this city, I thought it might be acceptable to your readers to hear what we there saw and heard. At about eight o'clock, in company with two friends, we repaired to the house. We had a pleasant reception by the medium and his amiable wife, and after a few minutes we were invited to the dining-room. And here let me say that the medium is a person well known to the business commmunity, and occupies a very responsible position in his business relations. The tablecloth was removed from a very plain table, nothing appearing about it more than was common for table purposes. A plain slate and some writing-paper was placed on the table; on the paper was placed just the smallest point of a lead pencil, nicely sharpened, and on the slate was placed a bit of pencil broken off by a pair of nippers. It was about the size of a big pin's head. Two tureen covers were brought, one placed over the slate, and the other over the paper. All being ready, the medium said he wished to make a few remarks before he proceeded further. He said he had been a skeptic as far as Spiritualism was concerned, and had, out of curiosity, been investigating these matters for ten or twelve years, and had come to the conclusion that there might be phenomena existing—something that has not as yet been explained by the ablest tests, or made comprehensible by the investigations of the most scientific men of the world, who had, a short time since, made a report which did not shed much light on the subject. He sometimes thought it might be animal magnetism, clairvoyance, psychology, psychic force, or some external subtle agency unknown to science, that produces, in certain conditions, results which are curious, interesting, and sometimes wonderful. He further said, that, as far as his experiments were concerned, he did not darken the room. Whatever might occur would be in the plain gas-light, which is entirely different in other sittings. He used these covers which answered all the purpose, it being comparatively dark under them, which was one of the conditions for a successful experiment.

"At this point we joined hands and remained in that situation for a few minutes. The medium asked one of the party to write some names on strips of paper — those that he wished to hear from that were dead. This person repaired to the next room, leaving the medium and two of us holding hands around the table. Soon he returned, and the medium, taking the slips of paper, folded up tightly, placed them on his forehead, when the visitor called the alphabet, which was made on a piece of paper, calling off A, B, C, and so on, until the letter was reached. For instance, in this case, as soon as the letter A was called, the medium said A; the next one reached was D, and he stopped at D, and so on, until the name of Adelbert was spelled out (never missing a letter), which was the name on the inside of the paper.

"But the next thing in the programme was perfectly unaccountable, and wonderful to behold. At this point, the medium announced that we were to have a communication in writing. Soon he told us to listen, and we did so, and to our astonishment heard distinctly the pencil moving under the cover, heard the dotting of the i's, and crossing the t's, and as the writing progressed it grew more distinct.

"All this time our hands were together,

and nothing but the two covers over the slate and paper were on the table, and only four of us present, and the room lighted. The writing ceased, the cover was removed from the slate and there appeared twelve or more lines, written in good style, and signed *Adelbert*. The composition was to the point, and referred to the evening's interview.

"An honest man with this result before him could not help but feel that he was in the presence of immortal beings, holding communication with those who inhabited the eternal regions of the hereafter—mortality holding converse with immortality—the agency being none other than the medium before us, a man.

"Soon after, the writer of this was requested to take a seat by the side of the medium, which he did. The slate was handed to him, with two or three little pieces of pencil, not bigger than the head of a big pin; they were placed on the slate. By the direction of the medium, the slate was placed under the table by the writer, and held tightly against the bottom of the table, with the medium's hand on the writer's hand. Very soon could be heard the movement of the pencil, and I could plainly feel the vibration. The sound was clear and distinctly heard by all.

"Soon the sound ceased and the slate was laid on the table, and there were four lines written in a bold and dashing hand, almost a fac-simile of the handwriting of the signer— the lines addressed to one of the company. This was equally as demonstrative as the other that there was no collusion, and that it was out of the power of mortal man to have produced it by his own agency. And while we were engaged about this last demonstration, the medium commenced rubbing his arm and called us to come close and see what was there. At first but little could be discerned, but it grew plainer and plainer, until letters stood out plain and distinct and spelled "Adelbert." It appeared like indentations in the skin ; no coloring, but white like the flesh. Again, during the evening in like manner, the name of "Mary" was spelled out, but nothing like as plain as the other name.

"Numbers of names were spelled out during the evening, and many little incidents were related by the medium, during the last ten or twelve years of his experience, in investigating this most curious of all curious subjects.

"We came away from our friend's house well pleased with our entertainment; if not a better man, certainly not a worse one."

As all of the persons attending the seance described in the foregoing article were my personal acquaintances, my spirit-guides desire me not to attempt an explanation of their methods of getting *en rapport* with me, at the time mentioned, fearing that the credit of the phenomena might be erroneously awarded directly to myself, instead of being given to my invisible controlling influences, where it justly belongs. I am allowed, however, to obey the impressions of a Diakka, who desires to lift the vail of mystery from one phase of the phenomena,—to wit, the names that appeared upon my naked arm. This Diakka claims to have controlled Charles H. Foster, hundreds of times, for precisely the same character of manifestations ; and he desires me to make public. the true science and *art* of this wonderful spiritual demonstration, believing that the world is now ripe for such knowledge. After I had become *en rapport* with the spirit of Adelbert, by a method similar to that practiced by Mr. Foster, which the Diakka will explain more fully hereafter, I adjourned the circle for a brief rest. During this interval, under the direction of my spirit-guides, I went into an adjoining room, and, with a large carpenter's-pencil, the point of which was nearly an eighth of an inch broad, I wrote, in bold letters, upon a plain piece of pasteboard, about double the thickness of a postal-card, the name,

With the sharp-pointed blade of a pocket-knife I then cut out the name, which I pasted, face downwards, upon a common playing-card. This gave me a regular stamp of raised letters, with the name reversed. Drawing up my sleeve, so as to leave my left forearm bare, I put the new-made stamp upon the fleshy part thereof, and replaced the sleeve. After we had reassembled in the circle, I soon felt impressed that the spirit of Adelbert desired to manifest itself by printing his name upon my arm. I therefore leaned heavily upon the table, pressing the left forearm upon the stamp for about thirty seconds, when the work was accomplished. I at once pushed up my sleeve, urging the card along with it, until I exposed the spot where the stamp had rested, when lo! the name "Adelbert" appeared as distinctly as it does upon these pages. The same Diakka which is now in control tells me that he has, for years, allowed a whole pack of playing-cards to remain in Foster's possession, upon each of which there is a common name, like Charles, Mary, Henry and John, in raised letters, all of which were manufactured in the manner I have described. These fifty-two names are arranged alphabetically, and are usually carried about the person of the medium, so that spirit-friends can, at a moment's notice, make their presence manifest by imprinting their earth-names upon the arm of their medium. The Diakka further states that Foster has another pack of cards, upon each of which appears a single raised capital-letter, which gives him a double alphabet. With the aid of these several dies, almost any spirit is enabled to imprint the initials of its earthly name as soon as it becomes fairly *en rapport* with its medium.

CHAPTER XV.

A SEANCE WITH DELEGATES FROM THE ONEIDA COMMUNITY.

DURING the winter of 1874-75, the Oneida *Circular*, a paper published by the Oneida Community of Central New York, contained a long letter, written by T. R. Noyes, giving an account of a sitting held at Syracuse with a gentleman who, as claimed by the writer, was not a professional medium, but merely a student of the science and philosophy of Spiritualism, who was accustomed, occasionally, to sit for his own improvement or the gratification of his friends. From Mr. Noyes' letter I make the following extract:

"We sat in the gentleman's dining-room, at an extension table, with two jets of gas brightly burning over it. One of his friends added to our circle made the number five. After asking us to select some spirit-friends who would be most likely to communicate, and write their names on slips of paper tightly folded, he, without opening the papers, put them to his forehead and spelled out the names. This proceeding was nearly identical with that pursued by the celebrated test-medium, Chas. H. Foster. Our host was somewhat slower, but equally successful after a time. Practice would undoubtedly make him fully equal to Foster as a test-medium in this line. But this was only preliminary to one of the most wonderful of the phenomena of Spiritualism, viz., direct slate-writing.

"Having, by means of the slips of paper and a half-hour's sitting, obtained a condition of *rapport* with us, and the spirits desiring to communicate, he produced a couple of ordinary slates, one of which was bound around the edge with black listing, to raise it slightly, and exclude light from its lower surface when laid on the table. Several small pieces were now broken from a slate-pencil with a pair of nippers. These pieces were small enough to move freely between the surface of the slate and the table, when the slate was laid over them. Both surfaces of the slate were next thoroughly cleaned with a sponge, and the slate was laid in the center of one the boards of the table, over the loose pieces of pencil. Some more of these were now sprinkled on the upper surface of the slate, and the other slate, also cleaned, laid upon it. On this were some more fragments of pencil, and covering these was an earthen tureen-cover.

"We then joined hands on the edge of the table; the gaslight was very slightly reduced, still remaining bright enough to read by easily. Presently the medium began to tremble, in the peculiar way always observed when strong phenomena are produced, and we heard the distinct scratching of a slate-pencil on a slate, coming from the pile of slates. The sound was unmistakable, and continued for some time. It then stopped, and, after a moment's silence, recommenced; this time, slower and more labored in its motion. All this while the medium's hands were on the table, touching those of each of his neighbors, fully ten inches from the slates, and in a good light.

"On examining the upper slate, nothing was found on it, nor upon the upper surface of the lower slate; but, on turning this last over, two communications of personal interest, signed by two of the spirits whose names had been spelled out, were found. One was to a gentleman present, who was a stranger to me. It was signed by the name of a friend of his who had died a year ago, and had promised to return if possible. It said, 'It is true, we *still live*. Have I kept my promise?' The writing was very beautiful, the delicate strokes showing the hand of a practiced penman. The deceased was a book-keeper, and the gentleman said the communication was a fac-simile of his writing.

"The other communication was to myself. It was longer, and of only personal interest. The writing was more labored and not recognizable as that of my deceased friend, although there were some points of resemblance.

"The most remarkable feature in this test, from a physical point of view, was the extreme delicacy and beauty of the writing from the spirit purporting to be that of the penman. The writing was done on the under side of the slate; consequently, the hand which did it was upside down. I think it would be difficult for any one to perform such writing without having his hand at ease in its accustomed position. Then, further, the space in which the writing was done was, at most, not over a quarter of an inch deep. If the hand was of ordinary size, which it must have been to get the natural stroke, it traversed the space occupied by the solid table-top without any interruption of its movement. Whichever way we view this fact it is equally amazing.

"After this we sat a few moments in the dark, and experienced the spirit-touches which are so common at dark circles. This gentleman seldom sits in the dark, preferring the light circle as more satisfactory. We left much pleased with the evening's entertainment."

As I am the person through whom the spirits manifested upon the occasion referred to by Mr. Noyes, I certainly ought to know whether he has correctly reported the sitting or not. I, therefore, cheerfully corroborate his testimony, so far as it goes, only regretting that he did not describe more minutely the various details of the seance.

I think, therefore, I may be pardoned if I again yield to the influence of a Diakka whose testimony I esteem as of great value, from the fact that he was one of my spirit-guides who assisted in producing the wonderful phenomena reported by Mr. Noyes. This Diakka inspires me to say:

"Mr. Noyes has given a very fair and truthful report of the manifestations *as they appeared to him*. He, however, describes only their results, leaving the process untouched. But what the world is now most anxious to know is, by what means can such results be obtained.

"That a spirit can, and does, communicate with those who are yet in the physical form, by writing upon a slate, and other methods, needs no confirmation. This is now one of the acknowledged facts connected with spiritual manifestations, as clearly and firmly established in the spiritual system as the power of gravitation is recognized by the scientific world. But just how the spirits can seize a slate-pencil and frame a comprehensible message, or by what precise means they influence a ponderable substance to move and convey intelligence to their earthly friends, is a question upon which even the spiritualists are divided. The true solution of this great mystery, up to the present time, is confined to a few persons, known to the world as great spiritual mediums. Thus the spiritualists, as a class, are at present clearly divided into two distinct and antagonistic factions— one wing comprising the few who *know* how the spirits work, while the other is made up of that vast army of spiritualists who do *not* know.

"For reasons heretofore explained, it has been thought unadvisable, hitherto, to attempt to unite these conflicting elements, but, instead, to allow each party to work in its own way for the general good of the cause. To-day, however, the whole civilized political and religious world is, in the words of Minot J. Savage, 'changing front.' Great rulers are fast beginning to realize that their power cannot long be maintained by simply attempting to hold the people in ignorance. The masses demand information upon all subjects, and, sooner or later, are determined to possess it. He who would exert an imperial influence upon the coming generation must place himself squarely upon the platform of universal education. The time will soon come when even the multitudes among the spiritualists who do not know will desire to ascertain the 'BOTTOM FACTS' connected with every spiritual manifestation. Already there are cases on record where individuals belonging to this category have asked important and pertinent questions, thus revealing the inclination to know something beyond what the average medium is allowed to tell; and unless the true science, as well as *art*, of all spirit phenomena is soon made manifest to these people—the very ones who support the great mediums—there will be danger of a rebellion from within, which would be likely to destroy the system altogether.

"If Spiritualism is to succeed in the future, it must grow, and, as the surest means of its growth, it is imperative that the laws governing spiritual phenomena should no longer be confined to the favored few, but be freely proclaimed to the world.

"When a spirit desires to write upon a slate, it invariably influences some susceptible person whom it can control, to do the writing in its stead. Heretofore it has been the custom of the spirits to influence the medium through whom they manifest to conceal the fact that they use his physical structure, and to make it appear to their friends that the spirits themselves perform the writing. This, however, is among the delusions which are no longer necessary, or advisable, to encourage. A spirit can not act directly upon any ponderable substance. Such a thing as a communication absolutely written by a spirit, without the aid of a physical, human hand, and the employment of material means, is an utter impossibility. Such a thing has never yet been accomplished, and, from my knowledge of spiritual laws, gained from a practical experience of more than twenty-five years, I fearlessly declare that it never can be."

So strong is my faith in the opinion of the Diakka now in control, that I am led to make the following announcement to the world: I hold myself in readiness, at any moment within the next twelve months, to enter into a contract with any honorable and responsible party, to pay any slate-writing medium in the world the sum of FIVE HUNDRED DOLLARS if he will induce a spirit to write, in my presence, a message containing three or more intelligible words, upon any slate, without the aid of some external and physical force. The main conditions of this offer are that all my expenses attending the experiment must be guaranteed, and I must be the last person who is allowed to examine the slate after the circle is formed, and before the writing is attempted.

During the day preceding the seance described by Mr. Noyes, which was held in the evening, the gentlemanly manager of the Oneida Community, Mr. F. Wayland Smith, called at my place of business in Syracuse, and asked me for the privilege of a sitting for himself and two other members of the Community. At first I flatly refused to comply with the request, telling him I was not a professional medium, but that I had seen enough to convince me that it would be a very poor investment for him to lose any time in seeking to solve the mysteries of Spiritualism. "The spiritual territory," I continued, "is full of quicksands. The investigator is liable to be swamped at any moment. Just when you think you have secured a key to some of its phenomena, *ignis fatuus* like, it eludes your grasp, and new and apparently more insurmountable obstacles mockingly present themselves." But Mr. Smith was not to be put off by trifling generalities. He informed me that the subject was then attracting a great deal of attention from some members of the Community, that a number had visited the Eddys, the Davenports, and several other noted mediums, all of whom referred them to me for independent slate-writing. This compliment proved too much for my spirit-guides, and they immediately persuaded me to reconsider my decision, which I did, making an appointment to receive the visitors at seven o'clock the same evening. The moment Mr. Smith left my office, I proceeded, under the direction of spirits who were anxious to get *en rapport*, to properly instruct a messenger, who followed Mr. Smith to his hotel (the Vanderbilt), where, by the aid of the register, they revealed to his physical eye the names of F. Wayland Smith and his whole party, male and female. On my way home, towards evening, I met an intimate, jocose friend, who, though not a believer, had long been desirous of witnessing some of the startling spiritual manifestations reported to occur in my presence. I invited him to attend the circle that evening, which invitation he readily accepted, saying that he should expect to hear from John Smith, who, he understood, had promised to come back from the spirit world, and show how closely he could imitate my own handwriting! The promise thus made by John Smith was—strange to say!—faithfully carried out, precisely as Mr. Noyes has described it. On the arrival of the party at my house, F. Wayland Smith readily gave me his own name, but asked to be excused, for the present, from revealing the names of his friends. I cheerfully assented to this arrangement, for, as will be easily imagined, I felt the influence of the spirits who had impressed the names of the others, by means of the hotel register, upon the physical eye of my messenger-boy. Suddenly turning to one of the party, I addressed him in a familiar way, by his given name, saying, "My spirit-friends tell me that an introduction to you is wholly unneccessary, as they can give me your name as easily as Miss —— (speaking the full name of the only lady in the party) could introduce herself." A revelation from the spirit-world so unusual and convincing took them all completely by surprise. This first handful of spiritual dust dimmed their vision to such an extent that the matter of getting in further *rapport*, by means of exchanging ballots, duplicating slates, and the like, was very easily accomplished by my spirit-guides.

CHAPTER XVI.

LETTER FROM L. W. CHASE.

THE Syracuse *Daily Courier* published, on the seventh day of December, 1872, the following graphic account of a seance given by me to an entire stranger, Mr. L. W. Chase, of Cleveland, Ohio, who reported the same for that paper :

"I notice with great pleasure that you have recently opened your columns to a correspondent who writes upon the subject of Spiritualism, and, hoping that the long-looked-for epoch has arrived when men of intelligence are willing to read and think upon this great subject, notwithstanding it may conflict with their old established belief or creed, and thinking that further evidence in this direction will be acceptable to you, as well as interesting to your readers, I beg to relate a little of my own experience. While sojourning in your city, a short time since, I learned that a gentleman, whom I will designate as 'Mr. T.,' was possessed of most remarkable clairvoyant powers, and that startling revelations from the spirit-land were almost a daily occurrence in his presence. I determined not to let so good an opportunity to investigate my favorite subject escape me. I made bold to call upon this individual at his residence. I need not say that I had many misgivings on introducing myself to this singular individual, for he was not at all like the person I had expected to meet. Mr. T. is a shrewd business man of, perhaps, thirty or thirty-five years of age, rather pleasant and gentlemanly in his manners, but cold and material in his reasoning, exceedingly skeptical in all matters of religious faith, and what the world would call an infidel. After learning my business Mr. T. inquired "Do you *believe* in the existence of spirits, and their communication with the living?' On my assuring him that I was already convinced upon that point, he remarked, 'Then why do you come here?' But before I could collect my thoughts to reply, he asked me to be seated, and, taking my hands in his own, I immediately began to feel that there was more than ordinary power in the man who sat before me. After remaining in this position for twenty minutes or more, Mr. T. requested me to go into an adjoining room and write down the names of several of my spirit-friends on bits of paper, and to fold them up tightly. I did as requested, and, on re-entering the room, he called out, 'This is all fraud; Caroline C—— *is not dead, but your sister Charlotte is.* If you wish to get anything at all, you must deal honestly with me.'

"Imagine my chagrin at being detected in this little deception, for *every word uttered by Mr. T. was true.* I had written the name of my friend C., who is yet alive; not to deceive the medium, however, but merely as an experiment. I am entirely satisfied that no mortal eye save my own rested upon the names I had written, and still held tightly folded in my hand, nor did a live soul in the city of Syracuse know the relations of these individuals to myself.

"The medium then took up a common slate, and, after carefully washing off either side, placed it flat upon the table, with a bit of pencil, about the size of a pea, underneath. We then joined hands, and, after the lapse of about ten minutes, under the full glare of gaslight, we could distinctly see the slate undulate, and hear the communication that was being written, a copy of which I herewith append :

"'MY DEAR BROTHER :—You strive in vain to unlock the hidden mysteries of the future. No mortal has faculties to comprehend infinity.   CHARLOTTE.'

"The above lines were not only characteristic of my beloved sister while in the form, but the handwriting so closely resembled hers that, to my mind, there cannot be a shadow of doubt as to its identity.

"Some clean white paper and a short lead pencil were now placed upon the table, and, after turning down the gas so that they were just visible to the eye, we again joined hands to await further developments. Directly the whole room seemed to shake violently. I distinctly felt something like a hand laid upon my head, and, before my eyes, the paper began to move around the table, in a circular manner, for several minutes, when suddenly it stopped and we heard the pencil fall. On turning up the gas, a short communication from my mother (and in her own handwriting) was found plainly written upon the paper.

"Many of your readers will doubtless be very skeptical in regard to the truth of these statements, but I believe the time is not far distant when the whole civilized world can witness for themselves so many absolute proofs of spirit communication with those in the form that to *doubt* upon this subject will not only evince greater credulity than to believe, but will necessarily destroy all confidence in our senses.

"I think, Mr. Editor, if men of science are anxious to investigate (in an honest manner) the subject of spirit phenomena, here is an excellent opportunity for such labor; here is a man who is not a professional medium, yet he is clearly subject to control by spirit-power, and seems willing to devote a good share of his time gratuitously to the development of this great truth. "Yours,
"L. W. CHASE.
"CLEVELAND, December 4, 1872."

More than ordinary weight should be attached to evidence of the foregoing character, from the fact that Mr. Chase was, as has been represented, an entire stranger to me; hence there could have been no collusion between us, and no reason could have existed why he should magnify or misrepresent the details of the seance. From my own recollection of Mr. Chase, I should say, without reservation, that he was an honest, earnest, seeker after spiritual knowledge. His report is, certainly, a straight-forward, unprejudiced one, and must force every candid investigator to the conclusion that no fair explanation of the phenomena can be given except upon the hypothesis that they were the direct communications of disembodied spirits. For ten years, Mr. Chase's story has slumbered peacefully in the minds of the people, no one having shown the courage, or even the disposition, to doubt its truthfulness, until to-day. The moment I began its resurrection, a number of Diakka seemed fairly to boil with indignation. Several of them formally entered their protest against the publication of the story in this work, while others reluctantly consented, upon condition, however, that I supplement it with their antidote. I am well aware that there are two sides to nearly every story; therefore, in simple justice, I will quietly yield to the influence of one member of the band, a Diakka who was present at the seance described, and who assisted in manipulating the unseen forces. Under his inspiration, and solely upon his responsibility, I will now proceed with the other version. The seance referred to was held at my house on an evening in the early portion of December, 1872. During the afternoon of the same day, just as I had closed business and was about to leave my office, Mr. Chase called upon me, for the first time, and requested a sitting. I flatly refused to entertain the proposition, giving, among other reasons, the fact that I was not a professional medium, but merely an amateur, investigating spiritual matters principally for my own amusement and instruction. The more excuses I offered for not wishing to entertain him, the more earnestly he begged that I would reverse my decision. I told him that nearly all of the current reports regarding the extraordinary character of the manifestations occurring in my presence were greatly exaggerated, and that it was more than probable that science would, at no distant day, reveal the true origin of the phenomena as being of a material, instead of a spiritual, nature. But all to no purpose; he had come determined to make an engagement for a sitting, and he pleaded with such persistency, that there seemed to be no reasonable way of escape for me. I had noticed, during our conversation, that he carried a large diary, in which he made one or two memoranda, and then replaced it in his overcoat pocket. While meditating as to the best means of disposing of this case, I was seized by a deep impression that the spirits could easily put me *en rapport* with this individual if I could, by any means, come in possession of that diary. We were sitting beside a large coal-stove, which radiated a good deal of heat, but not quite enough to cause my visitor to shed his overcoat. So I proceeded to turn on all the drafts, and shake down the fire, after which I resumed my seat, continuing to entertain the stranger according to the best of my ability. It was not very long before the perspiration began to start upon us both, when Mr. Chase arose and removed his heavy outer garment, placing it behind him on an empty chair. A moment after, I invited him into my private office, to look over some interesting works pertaining to the subject under discussion. While he was thus deeply engaged, I excused myself, for a moment, and, passing out of the hall door, came around to the main office, where the Diakka who now has control made a hasty examination of the diary already mentioned. Among the valuable information secured by this piece of strategy was that connected with a letter written, but a few days previous, by his sister, Caroline Chase, in which she mentioned the name of their deceased sister Charlotte. She also described a short and unsatisfactory seance which she had recently held with some professional medium, and closed by urging her brother not to pass through Central New York without visiting "the great Syracuse medium," alluding to my humble self. As soon as the Diakka had finished reading this letter, he replaced it, together with the diary, in the overcoat pocket, and, under his direction, I straightway returned

to Mr. Chase, pursuing the same route by
which I had left him. I then closed an appointment
with him for a sitting at my own
house, on the same evening, at seven o'clock,
and, giving him my street and number, we
parted. Thus ended our first meeting, which
Mr. Chase evidently entirely forgot, or did not
regard of sufficient moment to report, but
which, to the spirits, was the hour in which they
did their finest stroke of work.

At the appointed time, Mr. Chase arrived,
and the seance opened substantially as he has
stated. After sitting at the table for twenty
minutes or more, in order to get *en rapport*
with the spirits, I requested Mr. Chase to go
into an adjoining room, to write on slips of
paper the names of several deceased persons,
and to fold the ballots thus inscribed in such a
manner that their contents could not possibly
be seen by myself. He did so, and, on his
return, I saw that he had three ballots in his
hand. During his absence I had prepared
several blank ballots—the exact counterparts

of the ones upon which he had written—and had placed them in my left, outside coat-pocket. I now palmed three of the blanks in my left hand, and asked Mr. Chase to place his ballots upon my forehead. Under the pretext of holding them fast, I raised both my hands, palming his three ballots with my right hand, while, at the same time, I dexterously put the blanks in their place. I then carelessly lowered my right hand, and deposited the ballots containing the names in my lap. While Mr. Chase was engaged in pointing out the letters of the alphabet upon a printed card, my trusty dexter fingers opened the written ballots, and the spirits, through my gross and prying physical eyes, read their contents, which proved to be the names of his mother and the two sisters previously referred to. When the spirits learned that Mr. Chase had been trying to deceive them, by writing the name of his living sister, they were highly indignant, and, through me, exclaimed, "This is all a fraud! Caroline Chase is not dead, but your sister Charlotte is. If you wish to get anything at all, you must deal honestly with me." Of course, Mr. Chase humbly apologized for what he had done, and, during his embarrassed efforts to soothe the spirits, I again changed the ballots, adroitly palming the duplicates, and throwing the originals upon the table before him—he little thinking that they had been opened; for, in his published report, he declares that the ballots were read while he still held them tightly folded in his hand.

Previous to the arrival of Mr. Chase I had purchased two common slates, which were, to all appearance, exact duplicates. Upon one of these I wrote the communication referred to, and signed thereto the name "Charlotte." I then put this slate on the bottom of a chair, which I afterward occupied during the sitting, with the side bearing the communication next the seat, and covered it with a cushion, leaving the clean slate in plain sight upon the table. When impressed by the spirits that "Charlotte" wished to give her brother an exhibition of the marvelous power called independent slate writing, I took up the clean slate—*a la* Doctor Slade —in my right hand, and, after carefully wiping each side, as stated by Mr. Chase, I carelessly stooped a little, at the same time dropping my right hand, ostensibly for the purpose of drawing my chair nearer to the table, but really for quite another purpose. I here let go of the clean slate, and brought up the duplicate, which I laid upon the center of the table, with the message upon the under side. If Mr. Chase saw the movement at all, it did not excite his suspicions, as it was a perfectly natural one, and of very brief duration. I then dimmed the gas-light a trifle, and, raising the slate slightly, under the pretext of putting more bits of pencil beneath it, passed the loop-end of a fine oak-colored silk thread over the farther corner of the slate, the other end of the thread being already attached to a button of my coat. A moment after, I sat down, and, joining hands with the investigator, immediately experienced the severe nervous, trembling sensation which is common to all true mediums when great spirit-phenomena are produced. This motion of my body drew, of course, upon the thread, which caused the slate to move, apparently without physical force. I saw that Mr. Chase was intensely interested, so I released one of his hands and requested him to put it upon the slate; but, just as he was about to do so, the slate fairly leaped towards me, when the thread slipped off, leaving it entirely free from all material influences! Everything was now in good working-order for the forces to write upon the slate, with the exception of arranging the implements to produce the requisite sounds. This has heretofore been one of the most inexplicable mysteries connected with slate-writing. The Diakka says: "It is an easy matter to deceive the physical eye alone, and it is no difficult task to delude the gross material ear; but he who succeeds in misleading them both, is a necromancer qualified to capture a saint." I now slily took from my coat pocket a little wedge-shaped wooden clamp, in the lower end of which was permanently fastened a short piece of slate-pencil. This clamp I crowded

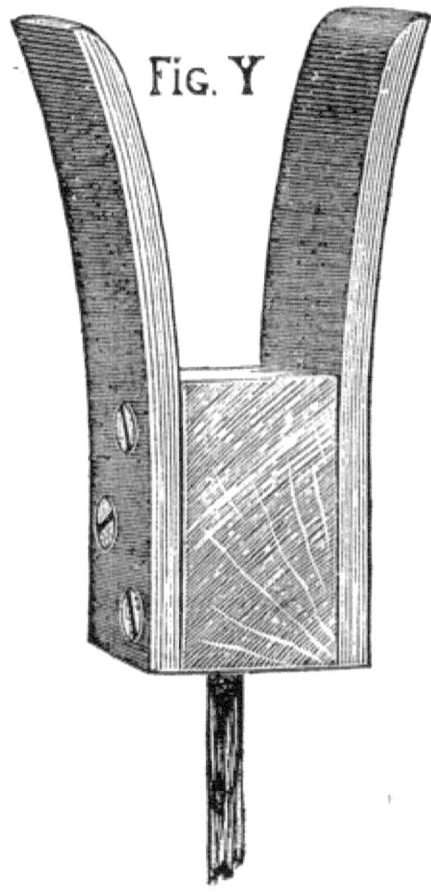
Fig. Y

upon the lower chime of the table, and putting a long slate-pencil through two little loops, made from sewing-silk, on the knee of my trowsers, I thus completed the mechanical arrangements of the mysterious process! We then joined hands, when I began to move my knee, rubbing the two pencils together in such a manner as to simulate the sound of writing upon a slate. (See Figure O, page 203.)

There are seven different methods by which the spirits impress their mediums to produce this startling phenomenon, all of them marvelously delusive, but the one here illustrated is probably the very best. I am told that Doctor Slade is frequently influenced to produce the sounds in this manner, when the spirit desires to communicate from the center of the table. For one unfamiliar with this science, to correctly locate the sound of writing, in the circumstances I have described, is almost an impossibility. Wherever the physical eye tells him that the writing may be expected to occur, there will the sound appear to be located. This defect in the physical ear can be readily demonstrated by the following simple experiment: Let four or more individuals sit around a common wooden table, each person being provided with two slate-pencils. Proceed to blindfold one of the party, so that he cannot discern even the smallest ray of light. Then let any one of the others place the end of a slate-pencil anywhere upon the table, while he rubs it lightly with another pencil, in imitation of writing, and see how difficult it will be for the party who is blindfolded to designate the particular person who produces the sound, or to declare from what part of the table it proceeds.

At the conclusion of the writing, while Mr. Chase was deeply engaged in reading "Charlotte's" remarkable and convincing communication, I wrote, by direction of my spirit-guides, a similar message, with a lead-pencil, upon a piece of white paper, to which I signed his mother's name. To one corner of this paper I attached, by a small white wafer, the end of the fine silk thread already used, the other end of which, it will be remembered, was tied to a button on my coat. These movements were all made in an easy and unconcerned manner, which can only be acquired by persistent practice. The light was now turned down quite low, and the paper upon which I had written was placed, with half a dozen other sheets, upon the center of the table, accompanied by a small piece of lead-pencil, as described by the investigator, when we again joined hands to await the further action of the spirits. It was not long before the whole room began to vibrate, as it would if I had put my foot under the table, resting it upon the ball, and had repeated the motion made by Mary Andrews, when the spirits desire to shake a room through her mediumship. A moment later, the papers began to quiver, and we could distinctly see one of the sheets move away from the others and proceed several inches towards the place where I was sitting. On turning up the gas, there appeared upon the most active sheet the following stereotyped message, the same which the spirits have, upon innumerable occasions,

Fig O
Spirits Writing in the Light.

repeated through Slade, Watkins, Phillips, Mansfield, Caffray, and other notable writing-mediums: "MY DEAR SON (or Brother, or Sister, or Friend, as the case may be): It is true that we still live and preserve our identity beyond the grave."

And these are the BOTTOM FACTS regarding that great seance which Mr. Chase admitted, at the time, was the most remarkable and convincing proof of immortality he had ever witnessed, during an active experience in spiritual research for more than a quarter of a century!

CHAPTER XVII.

THE PARAFFINE-MOULD TEST.

ONE of the most interesting and convincing among the many materializing experiments performed by our spirit friends, is the Paraffine-Mould Test, first introduced to the public through the mediumship of Mrs. Mary Hardy. This wonderful exhibition of their power was originally made by the spirits for the express purpose of causing it to appear to the doubting world that they could not only assume an earthly form by creating, or materializing, as it is commonly called, ghostly figures, but could leave, for future and critical inspection, an actual similitude of materialized hands, faces, feet and other parts of the human body. It was this phenomenon which aided, beyond everything else, in captivating that eminent geologist, Professor William Denton. That he was converted to the cause of Spiritualism through this particular manifestation alone, I am unprepared to state, but I am ready to testify that Professor Denton gave, at least, one public lecture in the city of Syracuse, almost wholly devoted to this subject, in which he fully indorsed Mrs. Hardy's mediumship, exhibiting, from the stage, some dozen or more plaster casts of human faces, heads and feet, which he unequivocally declared had been made from materialized spirit-forms by means of the paraffine process. The conversion of such a man as Professor Denton, was, at the time, a great triumph for the Spiritualists, for, through the class of manifestations so warmly indorsed by him, the cause has been elevated to a much higher plane than when the phenomena were confined to raps and table-tippings, and fully half of our mediums belonged to that lowest and most despicable of all orders, which claims to be controlled by the spirits of dead Indians.

But the world moves, and, with it, even every advanced and distinguished advocate of spiritual science must move also. While Professor Denton may have done good service to the cause, in the past, by proclaiming the naked fact that the spirits really manufacture the paraffine hands, &c., what the people now demand of him, and of those like him, is a full and intelligent explanation as to *how*, and by what method, the spirits produce this extraordinary result; nor will they be satisfied with anything less.

It was my good fortune to witness one of Mrs. Hardy's paraffine seances, held at the house of Doctor Wright, in the city of Washington, D. C., during the winter of 1876–77. We sat in a circle surrounding a plain wooden frame-work, about five feet square, constructed by fastening four strips of board together at the ends. This frame rested upon four legs, about two and one-half feet from the floor. A plain cloth was spread over it, reaching to the floor, which gave the whole structure the appearance of a covered table with curtains about it. A gentleman, who was introduced as Mr. Hardy, brought into the room a pail of hot water, upon the surface of which melted paraffine was visible, several inches in thickness. After carefully weighing the pail, and calling the particular attention of the audience to the operation, Mr. Hardy placed the pail under the center of the frame-work, at the same time requesting every member of the circle to witness that there was nothing there except the pail and its contents. We now joined hands, completing the circle. After engaging in divers songs, during which exercise Mrs. Hardy seemed to be very uneasy, a rattle of the bail of the pail was heard, which we were told indicated the close of seance number one. The curtain having been raised, there appeared beside the pail a thin paraffine-mould of a human hand. This, Mr. Hardy declared, had been fashioned by a materialized spirit, out of the paraffine in the pail—all of which he appeared to verify by again weighing the pail and its contents, together with the newly-manufactured hand, and announcing to those present that the aggregate weight was unchanged. Half an hour later, we re-assembled about the frame-work, forming three complete circles. On account of my recognized mediumistic qualities, (!) together with the display of a good degree of assurance, I was admitted to the inner circle, and placed nearly opposite the medium. A small aperture was now made in the center of the cloth covering the upper part of the frame-work, through which it was expected that the spirits would be able to show their materialized hands, &c. After sitting in this position for twenty minutes or more, I was fully conscious that the spirits were elevating Mrs. Hardy's foot to the aperture. A moment after, a number of voices exclaimed, "There it is! Look! See the spirit-hand!" An apparently fleshy substance could be indistinctly descried in the dim light, which the medium was able to convince some of those present was what it purported to be—a genuine materialized spirit-hand. Growing bolder by the success of each experiment, a few among those in the flesh were, at length, allowed, by the medium, to touch the spirit-hand. Fortunately, I was one of that honored number, and, when I reached into the aperture, I grasped —not a spirit-hand, but the *bare, material foot* of Mrs. Hardy! A sudden movement of her body induced me to squeeze the foot, for an instant, when, having caught her eye, which gave me a look at once imploring and despairing, I released my hold without exciting suspicion among the audience, simply saying, "I am satisfied." And I was satisfied that I had discovered the true key to the science and *art* of this materialized hand, and to the whole of the paraffine manifestations. Since then, I have been informed, by one of my spirit-guides, who claims to have formerly assisted Mrs. Hardy at her seances, that all paraffine hands, and other spirit moulds, are invariably formed *before the medium goes into the circle.*

The process is as follows : Take four or five pounds of common paraffine, and, having melted it, pour it into a pail half full of hot water—when the paraffine will rise to the surface. As soon as it has partially cooled, so that it will not burn the flesh, wash your hands in very strong soap-suds, and, while they are still wet, plunge one of them into the melted paraffine for a moment, and then withdraw it. Repeat this operation four or five times—just as our mothers used to dip candles—when a thin coating will cover the hand, showing its precise form so perfectly that even the exact appearance of the finger-nails can be readily recognized. Loosen this mould at the wrist, by means of an upward cut, when it can be removed as easily as a loose glove, but will retain its shape to perfection. Now close the cleft at the wrist, and cement the edges, by rapidly passing it over the blaze of a lighted lamp or candle, and afterwards smoothing it with your finger.

Having thus prepared a paraffine-hand, bend a common pin into the shape of a fish-hook, thrust this through the paraffine-hand, at the

THE PARAFFINE-MOULD TEST. 211

wrist, and thereby attach it to the leg of the left stocking, below the knee, at a point sufficiently high to insure its complete concealment by the skirts. Now cut off the toe of the stocking covering the right foot and put on a pair of slippers, or very loose shoes, and walk boldly into the circle. Sit down, as Mrs. Hardy did, between two trusty female friends, and, when a sufficient time has elapsed to allow the loss of water by evaporation to equal the weight of the paraffine-hand—which can be determined by previous experiment—shake off the right slipper and, with the bare toes, remove the paraffine-hand and place it beside the pail. Then rattle the bail and close the seance—for here endeth the Paraffine lesson.

CHAPTER XVIII.

THE WONDERFUL EDDYS.

AMONG the materializing mediums who are recognized by the whole spiritual fraternity as belonging to class Number One, are the Eddys, of Chittenden, Vermont. Twenty years ago or more, when these remarkable individuals first began to gain notoriety, the whole family consisted of ten members: Zephaniah Eddy, his wife and eight children—Miranda, James, Francis, Mary, Delia, Webster, William and Horatio. The survivors, at the present time, are, I believe, Zephaniah and his five last-named children. While the whole family, with the exception of the father, have been claimed as mediumistically inclined, the most famous of them all are William and Horatio. If a tithe of the exploits of our spirit-friends, through these brothers, during the last twenty years, could be written out, the record would fill many volumes. Although the most convincing proofs of their mediumistic qualities are reported to have been furnished at their country home,—where, it is alleged, the power is strongest, on account of the continual presence of their spirit-mother,— nevertheless William and Horatio, with the assistance of one sister, have given public exhibitions in many of our large cities, settling for thousands the great question of immortality— while hundreds of thousands of those who are numbered among the skeptical have been utterly confounded at their marvelous exploits. Like many other good mediums, however, these brothers are reported to have fallen into temptation, at least upon one occasion, and to have yielded to the natural appetite for filthy lucre, or, more probably, to the seductive voice of a fascinating Diakka, by giving genuine exhibitions of spirit-power, and palming them off upon a skeptical public as an *exposé* of spirit phenomena. But this little episode in the lives of these truly wonderful mediums does not appear to have seriously injured the cause, and it is, by no means, certain that it has in any degree militated against the mediums themselves, since the irrepressible Diakka who was evidently in control at the time did not attempt to expose any but that low and silly order of cabinet manifestations purporting to emanate from defunct Indians—the mere low-comedians and acrobats of the spiritual system.

Even though over-critical and unappreciative antagonists could, however, establish it as a fact that the so-called *exposé* was the direct and unassisted work of William and Horatio Eddy, this circumstance cannot be said to damage the cause itself in the smallest particular, for we can confront every skeptic with this incontrovertible logic, (our stereotyped answer), that a counterfeit does not destroy the original which it simulates, but absolutely proves its existence. The alleged evidences of charlatanism exhibited by these mediums, while under

Diakka influence, at their own home, which purported to emanate from the spirits of mischievous and saltatory Indians; the ridiculous antics performed by William, when disguised as an old squaw, with a dirty pipe, full of tobacco, in her mouth; the silly capers of Horatio, which he concluded by jumping upon a platform-scale to allow his spirit to be weighed —a process which is said to have converted poor Alcott—all this trifling is not worthy of consideration in these pages or elsewhere.

Fortunately, the Diakka have left us quite enough of the true and the genuine in connection with these very exhibitions, to convince even the most skeptical and self-opinionated that "there is life for all beyond the grave."

The grandest and, by far, the most convincing of all phases of spirit-phenomena ever exhibited through William and Horatio Eddy relate to what is known as the Curtain-test, in the light circle. These manifestations are particularly adapted to the convenience of mediums, both for their entire simplicity and the fact that they can be made to occur, under proper conditions, in almost any public hall or private drawing-room. Several times during the last fifteen years, it has been my good fortune to witness these peculiar evidences of future life, and, upon one occasion, I had the pleasure of sitting with one of the Eddy mediums before the curtain, and of being held by him while spirit-manifestations were in progress behind our backs. The manner of conducting this wonderful circle, by means of which so many have been converted to the cause of Spiritualism, is as follows: Either a cabinet is used, or a spirit-room is constructed by simply hanging a thick dark-colored curtain across one corner, or end, of the room where the exhibition is to be made. This curtain should be about eight feet long, having an aperture, twelve by eighteen inches square, in the center, and should be suspended at a sufficient altitude to prevent any person from looking over it; leaving the aperture about three and one-half to four feet from the floor. Directly behind this opening, and within two feet of it, is placed a small table, loaded with various paraphernalia used by the spirits in their manifestations— such as bells, rings, canes and musical instruments.

Three persons, including the medium, are then seated directly in front of the curtain, having their backs as close to the same as possible. Some elderly individual, whom it is desirable to convert to the cause, is usually honored with a position in the center of the group. This individual is required to place his hands upon his knees, and to remain in that position during the entire seance. The medium is now seated at his left, and grasps his left arm with both hands, while some one who is faithful to the cause is placed upon the opposite side, to perform a similar service—as shown in Figure A., p. 218.

In grasping the left arm of the party in the center, the medium uses his left hand first, spreading the fingers and thumb as far as possible. While pressing hard with the left hand, he takes a light hold with the right, covering, at the same time, a portion of the left.

If care is used, and the injunctions of the spirits are strictly obeyed, in making this grip, no person on earth can, from the sense of feeling alone, detect the withdrawal of the medium's right hand.

All of the preliminary arrangements are made in plain view of the entire assembly, and under strict conditions established by the spirits in control.

A second curtain is now hung in front of the trio and pinned about their necks—as shown in Figure B., page 221, for the alleged purpose of cutting off the magnetism of the physical eye, which is known to be antagonistic to spirit-power—often wholly neutralizing it.

By direction of the person in charge of the seance, a committee is now selected from the audience, with instructions to inspect every part of the spirit-room, in order to prove the fact to the most skeptical that no one is concealed within its sacred precincts, and that, consequently, no possible explanation of the expected phenomena can be given, except upon the hypothesis of spirit-power. After a satisfactory report of the committee has been rendered, they are remanded to their seats with the audience. A sitting of fifteen or twenty minutes, interpersed with singing, "John Brown's body lies mouldering in the grave," or some equally appropriate ditty, usually follows, when a slight agitation of the little curtain at the aperture indicates that sufficient *périsprit* has been generated to enable the spirits to manifest themselves. At first, these demonstrations are very faint ; a confused, rustling sound is heard behind the curtain, as if some one was arranging the instruments upon the table ; this is followed by the faint tinkle of the smallest bell, when every sound, save the heart-beats of the anxious audience, is hushed, and painful stillness reigns supreme. A few minutes later, a loud noise is heard within the cabinet, indicating that some ponderous substance has fallen upon the floor ; two or three bells are rung at the same moment ; the tambourine is violently played upon, while plainly visible at the aperture ; every member of the trio receives a slight blow from the tambourine upon the head— when the hubbub momentarily ceases, and the tambourine falls in front of the curtain. Then an invisible agency raises the guitar in full view

of the audience, while chords are played upon it; a heavy iron ring is thrown over the shoulders of the investigator, and a bell is placed upon his head by the same influence; several hands are exhibited at the aperture, which, in the dim light, can be easily recognized as belonging to the spirits of at least three distinct races. One hand, as black as Erebus, is seen just above the top of the curtain, while, at the same time, a white hand appears at the aperture. An infinite variety of similar manifestations follows, until the spirits seem to be exhausted, or the audience becomes surfeited, when the same old trembling sensation passes over the medium, which is plainly noticeable to the assembly, and the seance closes. An attendant now unpins the outer curtain, which drops to the floor, revealing the trio in exactly the same positions which they occupied at the beginning of the seance, as represented in Figure A.

I am not allowed, by my guides, to close this chapter without submitting to the control of a friendly Diakka, who desires more fully to explain the science and *art* of the Eddy phenomena, by giving the public a peep behind the curtain during their occurrence. I have great confidence in this Diakka, from the fact that he has been constantly in the service for the last quarter of a century, assisting the Eddys, the Carbonells, the Fays, the Snell Brothers, the Davenports, and many other celebrated mediums, in producing the identical phenomena I have just described. Under his influence, I will therefore proceed.

Before seating himself in front of the curtain, Horatio Eddy, by direction of the spirits, supplies himself with not a little requisite paraphernalia, which is secreted about his person. The moment the front curtain is raised, which cuts off the magnetism of the physical eye, the medium's right hand is removed from its position upon a part of the left without being detected by the person upon whose arm his hands are resting. The spirits then employ this physical right hand to ring the bells, handle the iron rings, agitate the tambourine and thrum the guitar, as shown in Figure C.

A number of stuffed gloves, of various shades and sizes, are now taken from the person of the medium, and shown at the aperture for an instant, which, in the dim light, are readily mistaken, by the audience, for spirit hands. The old cane with a crooked handle, which is carelessly left upon the table, within easy reach of the medium, often serves a better purpose than to assist the spirits of dead Indian cripples in their new attempts at locomotion. With this cane in the medium's right hand, the spirits can magnetize a chair, or almost any light piece of furniture standing anywhere behind the curtain, within a radius of five or six feet, so that they can show it at the aperture, and then replace it at the farthest corner of the room. They can also utilize the cane to elevate a dark-colored glove above the curtain, at the same moment when the hand of the medium, which grasps the lower end of the cane, is plainly visible at the aperture. Thus the spirits are able to exhibit to the audience the materialized hand of a negro and a white man at the same instant, the different hands being so far apart as to preclude (in the judgment of the witness), the suspicion that the medium is accessory to the manifestations. In case the committee, while examining the apartment, before the seance begins, are too officious, and attempt to destroy the conditions by placing the table and its contents beyond the reach of the medium, the spirits are not thereby necessarily disconcerted. If the cane is left to them, they can easily hook the handle about the leg of the table and draw it back within the power of their *périsprit*. In the absence of the cane, they take from the medium's pocket what is termed by the spiritualists a "grab-all," and therewith quickly accomplish the same result. A grab-all consists simply, of two pieces of lead, weighing about one ounce each, fashioned in the shape of an anchor. One of these is tied to each end of a stout cord, about one foot in length, and to the

226   THE WONDERFUL EDDYS.

middle of this ligature is attached a string long enough to reach to any part of the spirit-room.

A loop is formed in the end of this cord, and the toy is coiled up, ready for use. When the spirits find their medium "pickled," in the manner just intimated, they induce him to put his hand through the loop and let the anchors fly in the direction of the table. As the leads spread apart in their flight, and since there are four legs to the table, one or two casts of the grab-all will be sufficient to capture it. When the table has been thus secured, the medium raises one side of it a trifle, so that the grab-all will slip off, after which the spirits have it all their own way, and great is their power and marvelous are their manifestations!

CHAPTER XIX.

ROPE-TYING TESTS.

NOT the least among the many striking physical proofs of spirit-power, are what is known as the rope-tying tests, introduced at an early period in the history of modern Spiritualism, by that celebrated medium Henry Melville Cummings Fay, of Akron, Ohio.

For more than a quarter of a century, this peculiar phase of spiritual manifestations has survived the deliberate and persistent assaults of a skeptical public and a prejudiced press, and, at this moment, stands as firm as Gibraltar.

A seance for the exhibition of this phenomenon is usually conducted in the following manner: The medium through whom manifestations are expected to occur is, first, securely tied with strong cords, or ropes, by a committee of experts selected from the audience. Afterward, he is placed within a cabinet, if one is at hand, otherwise, the lights are extinguished and total darkness reigns. This is done in order—as has often been stated in this work— to cut off the power of the physical eyes, it being one of the conditions invariably demanded by the spirits, for this class of phenomena, that the medium through whom they operate must not be visible to the audience during the process of the manifestations.

No matter how expert the committee may be, or how securely they may bind the medium, within ten or fifteen minutes after he has passed from their sight, every rope will mysteriously fall from his person!

When restored to the gaze of the spectators, the medium walks forth free and untrammeled with the untied ropes in his hand, thereby clearly demonstrating to them the presence of spirit-power.

When darkness again overshadows the

medium, the spirits proceed to tie him, in the most intricate manner, to his chair, apparently rendering him far more secure than he was when bound by human hands.

A small table, laden with musical instruments and other paraphernalia, is now placed near the medium: instantly bells are rung, horns are blown, phosphorescent lights appear, a guitar is played upon, while apparently floating in the air, and, for a time, Bedlam, itself, seems to have been let loose. When the medium is restored to the vision of the audience, he is found to be effectually tied to the chair, with his hands behind him,—the work having been done in such a manner as to render it impossible, in the opinion of the ordinary investigator, for him to have been instrumental in producing the extraordinary phenomena.

Henry S. Olcott describes a circle of this kind, given through the mediumship of Horatio Eddy, as follows: "The preparations for this event consist in having shawls, or blankets, hung over the four windows to exclude even star-light, removing the table, with its array of musical instruments, to a position on the main floor, just in front of the railing, and tying Horatio in a chair, placed to the right of the table and in front of the spectators. Upon the extinction of the light, the gruff voice of the sailor-spirit, George Dix, and the piping whisper of the little girl-spirit, Mayflower, are heard greeting us. . . . . Compliments being exchanged, a medley performance begins. There is a dance of a pack of howling, leaping, sky-larking Indians, who beat on the drums, rattle the tambourines, blow the horns, ring the heavier bells, and make a din so hideous that one easily fancies himself caught in the melee of a dance of live redskins, about starting on the war-path. If Horatio were unbound and using all four of his locomotive and prehensible members, he could not imitate this dance. The creatures yell and one can hear their stamping on the floor in cadence with their rude music.

The dance is preceded by a stillness so dead

that, for any sound of life, we might fancy the room empty.

A slow beating of the time, a few clangs of the big dinner-bell, a measured beat of the tambourine, and the time grows faster and faster until, in a moment, we are in the midst of the hurly-burly. It needed no stretch of imagination to see, in the Egyptian darkness of the hall, the wild figures circling round and round, for their demonstrations were of so obstreperous a character as to frighten all but *habitues* of the coolest temperaments.

As an exhibition of pure brute force, if such a term may be applied to the occult power that produces it, this Indian dance probably is unsurpassed in the annals of spiritual manifestations."

The true science and *art* of all spirit phenomena exhibited through the rope-tying test, revealed to me by my spirit-guides, after twenty five years of investigation, and much practical experience, are as follows :

Before entering the seance room, every

BEFORE THE DARK SEANCE.

AFTER THE DARK SEANCE.

such medium, by direction of his controlling influences, provides himself with two sets of ropes, which are exact duplicates. One of these is concealed about his person, while the other is given to the committee who tie him. The medium is also provided with a short, sharp, open knife, which he places inside his wrapper-sleeve, near the arm-pit, with the blade pointing upward. This knife is kept in position by putting the lower end of it into a pocket, about an inch deep, prepared for the purpose by sewing a small piece of tape to the inside of the wrapper-sleeve. The knife is never used except in a case of extreme urgency. Not one person among a thousand, selected as committeemen at a spiritual circle, can tie a good medium, with the stiff cotton cords furnished him, so as, in any wise, to prevent the spirits from promptly setting him at liberty. The medium always manages, during the tying ordeal, by slight contortions of his body, to secure a little slack rope, by the agency of which the spirits can upset almost any square knot, readily converting it into a slip, from which one hand can be easily extricated—when the full release of the medium quickly follows. In case, however, the medium gets "pickled" by the committee, or, in other words, when the spirits find that they cannot, by any fair means, untie the medium,—which very rarely occurs,—as a last resort, they use the knife. By a slight movement of the medium's upper arm against the back of his chair, the knife is lifted out of its shallow pocket, and quickly slides down into the palm of his hand, when the rope is cut and the prisoner is free. The pieces of rope are now carefully concealed in the medium's pocket and the duplicates are brought forward to be exhibited to the mystified and credulous audience as the original ropes. The knots tied by our spirit-friends are almost as numerous in character as the mediums through which they are exhibited. They are all, however, offshoots of the three original knots, known as the "double-header," the "single-header" and the "great front-twist."

At present, I shall confine myself to an explanation of the first two; the great front-twist will be minutely explained and appropriately illustrated further on in these pages. The double-header is always used in the dark circle, or cabinet seance, where extraordinary phenomena are expected to take place, and the spirits demand the free and unrestrained use of the medium's body during their manifestations. A hard-laid cotton rope, or cord, about twelve feet long and one-fourth of an inch in

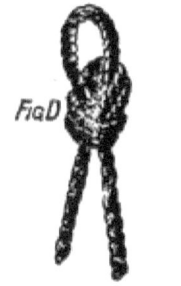 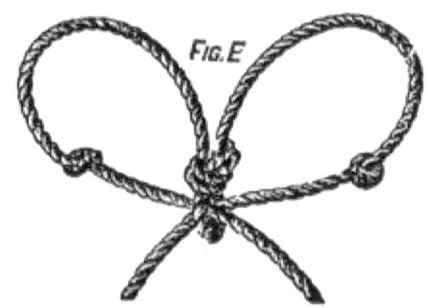

diameter, is tied at the centre in a plain bow-knot, as shown in Figure D, above A simple over-hand knot, called a header, is now tied in the same rope, on either side of the centre knot, at such a distance from it that the amount of rope between the two will exactly span the wrist of the medium. The ends of the rope are then tucked through the small loop, and tightly drawn, when the double-header is complete. See Figure E, page 235.

The single-header knot is tied in the same manner as the double-header, with this exception: the loop around the left wrist is permanently fastened, and does not slip. This knot is frequently used by the spirits in their front act, when they desire to apparently secure the medium's hands to his knees, and the manifestations do not require the use of both. It is a very good tie for this purpose, but nothing to be compared with the great front-twist. The rope is now securely tied, on either side of the double-header, to the back of a chair, while the ends are brought in front, where they are made fast to the lower round of the chair, of course quite beyond the reach of the medium. The

medium then seats himself in this chair, and, encircling the back with his arms, slips each hand through the loops—shown in figure E—and, straightening his body, both ropes slip until they reach the headers, which stop them just at the point where they are snugly fitted to the wrists, not being, however, drawn so tight as to impede the circulation of the blood. When the loop in the bow-knot (D) and the two headers are thus brought together in the centre of the rope, the whole appears very intricate and must be regarded as secure. The audience is now allowed to see the medium, and an examination on the part of the committee usually follows. The committee *invariably report the medium to be securely tied*, from the fact that the true character of the knot absolutely defies discovery, while the ropes are taught, and no good medium will ever allow the slightest slack in his bonds during such examination.

CHAPTER XX.

THE COTTON-BANDAGE TEST.

BY far the most interesting of all methods of securing mediums, in order to physically demonstrate the presence of spirit-power, is what is known as the "Cotton-bandage test," originally introduced to the public, about thirty years ago, by Miss Laura Ellis, who traveled with her father through many portions of the country, giving spiritual exhibitions to the multitude, thereby mystifying the skeptical and converting the credulous, by thousands, to the cause. Other lights of lesser brilliancy, like the Carbonelles, the Snell Brothers, and Warren Lincoln, have followed in the wake of this truly wonderful medium, demonstrating the same phase of spirit-power, under the same test conditions, but without creating a tithe of the excitement caused by the original exhibitor. For more than a decade after Miss Ellis had retired to private life, the cotton-bandage test practically disappeared from our public seances, for the sufficient reason that the spirits could find no medium competent to fill her place. When, however, any unusually urgent demand is made, by the public, for a person gifted with extraordinary powers, either in civil or military life, the world always fills the vacancy. The Revolutionary war gave to us a Washington and a Lafayette, while our own deplorable civil strife brought forth Grant, Sherman and Sheridan. The cotton-bandage test was of too great importance to long slumber in comparative oblivion. Hence the vast army of unseen spirits which constantly surround us called upon the world for a medium of surpassing accomplishments, through whom they could manifest, and bring nearer to perfection, this extraordinary phase of spirit phenomena—when lo! as if by magic, there appeared before us, smilingly presenting herself to the *savants* of this world, that rarely-gifted medium, ANNIE EVA FAY. This marvelous *debutant*, who was afterwards dubbed, by the scientists of Europe, "The Indescribable Phenomenon," probably made more rapid strides towards the attainment of notoriety as a medium than any other person who has ever existed. Born in an obscure town in the interior of Ohio, reared in poverty, with scarcely the advantages of a common-school education, we find this young woman, within a few months after her first development as a medium, giving spiritual entertainments, at half a guinea a head, to many of the first people in England, and creating a greater *furore* among the people of all classes than any medium who has ever left our shores. So remarkable were the spirit manifestations permitted to occur through this medium, that she readily secured the endorsement of members of the Royal Society, while scores of Lords, Dukes, and others of the nobility of England, were, through her, fully converted to the cause of Spiritualism. She rapidly made the personal acquaintance of many people in the higher walks of life, throughout the Continent, while the spirits manifested, through her, even in the presence of crowned heads, including the Czar of Russia and the Queen of England. William Crookes, F. R. S., fully tested the powers of this wonderful medium, by submitting her to a series of experiments in his own private laboratory. In the process of these experiments, he successfully used the galvanometer, tying the medium, by means of an electrical current, in such a manner as to render it apparently certain that she could not use her hands, or in any way assist the spirits to manifest, without interrupting the current which the galvanometer *is supposed* to record. After Professor Crookes became convinced that the spirit manifestations, through this medium, were genuine, he assisted her in exhibiting the phenomena, through the galvanometer, to other scientists, many of whom were, at the time, bewildered, although few, if any, were converted to the cause.

242   THE COTTON-BANDAGE TEST.

After a brief, but brilliant, career in Europe, this marvelous medium, armed with the endorsement of Mr. Crookes and other notables, returned to America, where, for several years, she gave private seances, with varying success, until the fall of 1879, when she and her manager, H. Melville Fay, began exhibiting to large houses throughout the United States and Canadas. Their performances were heralded by the following bill. the precise locality being, of course, omitted :

(SEE NEXT PAGE)

C. C. BRADDON

WILL GIVE A RELIGIOUS ILLUSTRATED

LECTURE OF SPIRIT POWER IN THE LIGHT,

ASSISTED BY

THREE OF THE BEST MEDIUMS IN THE WORLD,

INCLUDING THE CELEBRATED

ANNIE EVA FAY,

OF LONDON, ENGLAND.

The mediumship of Miss Fay has been subjected to the severest Scientific Tests by Prof. WM. CROOKES, F. R. S., and other prominent Scientists of England. Their frank endorsement gave her great popularity, and drew large audiences at the Crystal Palace, Sydenham; and, at the solicitation of her Majesty, Miss Fay filled the Queen's Court Rooms, Hanover Square, for eight consecutive weeks.

The following are some of the tests that usually take place in the presence of these mediums:

While the medium is raised from her seat and floating in mid-air, the many spirit forms that appear around her are truly wonderful, and seen by all present; they stand beside you, converse with you as in life, and shake hands with their friends. These are Genuine Mediums, endorsed by the press and the public wherever they appear.

A Table rises 4 to 5 feet and **FLOATS in MID-AIR.** Spirit Hands and Faces are plainly seen and recognized by their friends.

A GUITAR IS PLAYED and passed around the room by the invisible power. FLOWERS ARE BROUGHT and passed to the audience by hands plainly seen.

Bells are rung, Harps are played, and other tests of a startling nature take place in presence of these THREE WONDERFUL MEDIUMS.

A LARGE PIANO RISES CLEAR FROM THE FLOOR,

And is Played upon without a living soul touching it.

And many Spirit forms that appear upon the stage—sometimes eight or ten at a time—are proof positive of the genuineness of these Mediums. They have been three years developing for the special purpose of demonstrating the facts of

SPIRIT POWER IN FULL GAS LIGHT!

This is something new, and *never before attempted in this country.* Every opportunity will be given for the CLOSEST INVESTIGATION by the public press. Skeptics are especially invited to be present and occupy the Front Seats. These Mediums have been giving these

ILLUSTRATED LECTURES,

Throughout England and the British Provinces, and have just appeared in the United States.

CHALLENGE.

These Mediums challenge all exposers, including BISHOP, BALDWIN, HERMAN, HOUDON, HARTZ and STARR, none of which dare meet them.

The Invisible Powers are constantly producing New and Startling manifestations, to convert the skeptical and strengthen the unbeliever. COME AND SEE FOR YOURSELVES. Take no one's word! Investigate, and believe your own eyes. Be guided by your own reason.

EVIDENCE THAT THE DEAD DO RETURN.

Persons doubting the following assertions can write to the parties and substantiate the same:

LADY MAYHEW, No. 2 Vernon Place, Bloomsbury Square, London, states: "That thinking there might be some deception in the hall, took the mediums to her own house, no one present but her own family; that while herself and brothers were holding them, the guitar floated around the parlor, touching many upon the head; bells were suspended in the air and rung, and her mother appeared, and was seen by *all present;* that there was no chance for deception, as the medium had never visited the house before that day."

The COUNTESS OF CAITHNESS, of Landsdown Terrace, saw her husband; he stood beside her, conversed with her, placed his arms around her neck, and kissed her as in life.

H. B. GREENWOOD, No. 11 Angel Court, Throgmorton Street, London, stated: that he had never seen any manifestations, or even believed in Spiritualism, nor didn't know as he did now, but certainly there was something wonderful and miraculous in the manifestations; that his little grandchildren came to him, sitting upon his knee, placing their arms around his neck, called him "grandpa," and asking for "papa" and "mamma;" that he distinctly saw them as they were sitting there, and felt their presence upon his lap.

C. C. BRADDON, and mediums, held a seance last evening, at Steinway Hall, to a full house. The performances were new, and startling enough to almost, if not quite, convince the veriest skeptic. Spirits were seen, felt and heard; musical instruments were played upon by spirit hands; the mediums were securely tied and bound to a chair by the spirit of Muhlenburg, whose form was plainly seen by the entire audience. These are the only mediums through whom spiritual manifestations are developed in full gas-light.—*Spiritual Telegraph.*

MRS. WILLIAM CHASE, of New York City, testified to the audience, that she had not previously been in the presence of a spiritual meeting or medium, for twelve years, but on this occasion curiosity prompted her to see these mediums, and, on being seated with them, her mother, Mary, her sister Alice, and little child, Willie Lewis, appeared to her, and even talking to her, giving her many cheering and comforting messages.

DR. W. S. STEVENS, of No. 14 Arch St., Philadelphia, states: "I had C. C. Braddon and mediums in my own parlor, paying them $100 for a private seance, and none but members of my own family being present. Spirit forms appeared, as many as seven at once; they conversed with us, shook hands and played upon the piano, raising it to a height of three feet from the floor. We (myself and my family), were not believers in Spiritualism, nor had we ever seen any manifestations before. What I give here are simply facts, and I am positive that no deception could have been practiced, and that each manifestation was most thoroughly investigated. I would further state that the manifestations were all produced in full gas-light; and I do heartily recommend these mediums as ladies and gentlemen worthy the patronage of both the citizens of the British Provinces and United States, and I shall be pleased to answer any communications that may be addressed to me on this subject."

NEW YORK HERALD, January 25th: "Might truly be called a marvelous seance. The guitar was seen to rise in the air, while some invisible hand was thumbing it for a space of three minutes. The committee was allowed to hold the medium while the manifestations continued as before. It is inexplicable."

The NEW YORK TELEGRAM, December 31st, says: "It is fortunate for Miss Fay that she did not live in old Cotton Mather's time; psychic force would have been too thin an excuse for her, and not even Mr. Crookes, as attorney for the defense, could have saved her from being burned as a witch."

The NEW YORK GRAPHIC, December 31st, says: "Neither the committee or other spectators were able to fathom the mystery. Miss Fay was firmly tied to the wall and pinioned by a committee. Indeed the demonstration continued while she was held by a reporter of the *Tribune*."

LONDON STANDARD, July 5th: "Nothing half so bewildering has been seen in England. Quite beyond the range of description."

The LONDON DAILY TELEGRAPH, MARCH 12th, 1874. "*Science and Spiritualism.*—In the Spiritualist of yesterday, Mr. Wm. Crookes, F. R. S., prints an account of a seance at his house, in which Miss Fay exhibited some remarkable phenomena while under severe scientific conditions. The sitting took place on Friday evening, February 19th, in the presence of several well-known men of science, and, on Mr. Crookes' suggestion, the medium was so placed as to form part of an electric current connected with a galvanometer, indicating, on a graduated circle, the exact deflection produced by the current. In each hand Miss Fay held the terminal of a wire, and the fact that she kept continuous hold of the terminals was guaranteed by the amount of the deflection of the galvanometer needle, and by the flashes of light which accompany each change of position or break of contact. This method was agreed to by the savants present, as affording absolute certainty that the medium could not remove her hand or body from the wires, whether in a trance or otherwise, without the fact being made known by the galvanometer. The sitting was held in a well-lighted drawing room, the medium, thus 'tied down by electricity,' being screened by a curtain."

A SMALL ADMITTANCE FEE TO DEFRAY EXPENSES WILL BE CHARGED AT THE DOOR.

These bills are issued at the rate of one to every five inhabitants in the town where the seance is to be given. The city is thoroughly canvassed, for at least three days prior to the entertainment, and every dwelling, office and shop, within its area, receives its full share of attention. Long before the hour appointed for the spirits to begin their work, a large concourse gathers about the doors of the hall, and when, at last, the gentlemanly H. Melville Fay raises the wicket and announces, " Tickets only fifty cents to all parts of the house," there is a general scramble. An hour later, the largest Opera House is packed full of human beings, combining all classes, from the millionaire to the pauper. Every religious and irreligious phase of society is represented in the assemblage, all burning with eagerness to witness the many promised wonders.

When the curtain rises, Professor Braddon —*alias* H. Melville Fay—clad in faultless attire, appears upon the stage, and, bowing gracefully to the audience, begins the freely-advertised

"Religious Illustrated Lecture," in the course of which—doubtless under Diakka influence!—he plagiarizes, copiously and without conscience, from Swedenborg, Kardec, Hull, Davis, and other prominent spiritual writers, while, at the same time, he indulges in not a little original humor, sentiment and pathos. This lecture, lasting for half an hour or more, is termed, among show-people, the "time-killer," or the "mellowing process," and is intended to prepare the audience for a higher and more spiritual condition. The stage is usually arranged for a drawing-room scene, in the centre of which a cabinet is erected, consisting of four upright poles, about eight feet high, placed some six feet apart, and made fast to the floor by large screw-eyes. These poles are braced, at the top, by four horizontal bars, making a stout frame-work, about six feet square. This is covered with a thick, dark-colored cloth, and a curtain of the same material is hung on a wire in front, forming the door to the cabinet.

THE COTTON-BANDAGE TEST.

Annie Eva Fay now appears upon the scene, clad in rich attire, every detail of which betrays good taste and exquisite workmanship. Smiling on the assembly, in her most artless and bewitching manner, she proceeds to address them in about the following style : " Friends, we are assembled to-night, I trust, for a common purpose. You have seen our bills, and have read our advertisements, so there cannot be a shadow of doubt as to the object of your presence. You are here to be entertained, perhaps instructed, and possibly astonished. In order to witness manifestations at all satisfactory, it will be absolutely necessary for every person in this audience, to preserve the most perfect harmony and decorum, carefully observing every rule we have been necessarily compelled to establish. The success, or failure, of our entertainment lies wholly with you, as we cannot guarantee the support of invisible agencies unless every rule is strictly adhered to. I hope, therefore, that no one will be so rude, or so unmindful of the rights and wishes of those who really desire to investigate the wonders which are soon to appear, as to oppose, even with his will-power, the conditions which are indispensable in securing the anticipated manifestations. I trust that, on the contrary, all will co-operate with us in working for results which will be impressive, even if they fail to be convincing. Remember, we do not wish to proselyte any reluctant person to our faith. We believe that the extraordinary phenomena sometimes occuring in our presence are precisely what they purport to be—the efforts of disembodied spirits to make themselves consciously manifest, and to communicate intelligently with those who are still in the physical form.

"We are willing, however, that each one present should form an independent opinion, with reference to these phenomena, unbiased by any act or statement of ours. Many of you have, doubtless, come here expecting to witness every manifestation described upon our bills. To such let me frankly say, You will be disappointed. We have, simply, advertised a number of manifestations which usually occur. Doubtless, some of them will be omitted to-night, while new and startling disclosures, will take their place. Now, if there are any present who are dissatisfied with the conditions we are compelled to impose, in order that satisfactory phenomena may be witnessed, let them retire at once, before the entertainment really begins, and their money will be refunded at the door."

After this little sagacious speech, which excites the curiosity and whets the appetite of every listener, while, at the same time, it cunningly circumvents all chronic grumblers, on one was ever known to leave the house.

Two persons are now selected from the audience to inspect the cabinet, tie the medium, and assist the gentlemanly lecturer in conducting the seance, while, at the same time, they are expected to keep a watchful eye upon all occurring manifestations, in order to protect the public against imposition. The medium is now firmly tied about each wrist with a simple cotton bandage, about one and a half inches wide by half a yard in length. The committee usually tie these bandages in a plain double square knot, drawing each knot down tight, as shown in Figure L, page 252. Unlike the double-header, the great front-twist, or any other hemp or cotton intricacy with which mediums are wont to be afflicted, the cotton-bandage tie is designed by the managers of the seance to be permanent. As evidence of this fact, the committee are requested to sew the knots through and through, which they do, until fully satisfied that they are secure. The medium now places her hands behind her, and, so clasping them that her wrists are but six inches apart, politely requests the more nervous of the two committee-men to tie the ends of the bandages firmly together. After this has been accomplished, the dangling extremities of the bandages are cut off, and the last knot is sewed, if necessary, leaving the medium firmly bound, with a short ligature between her

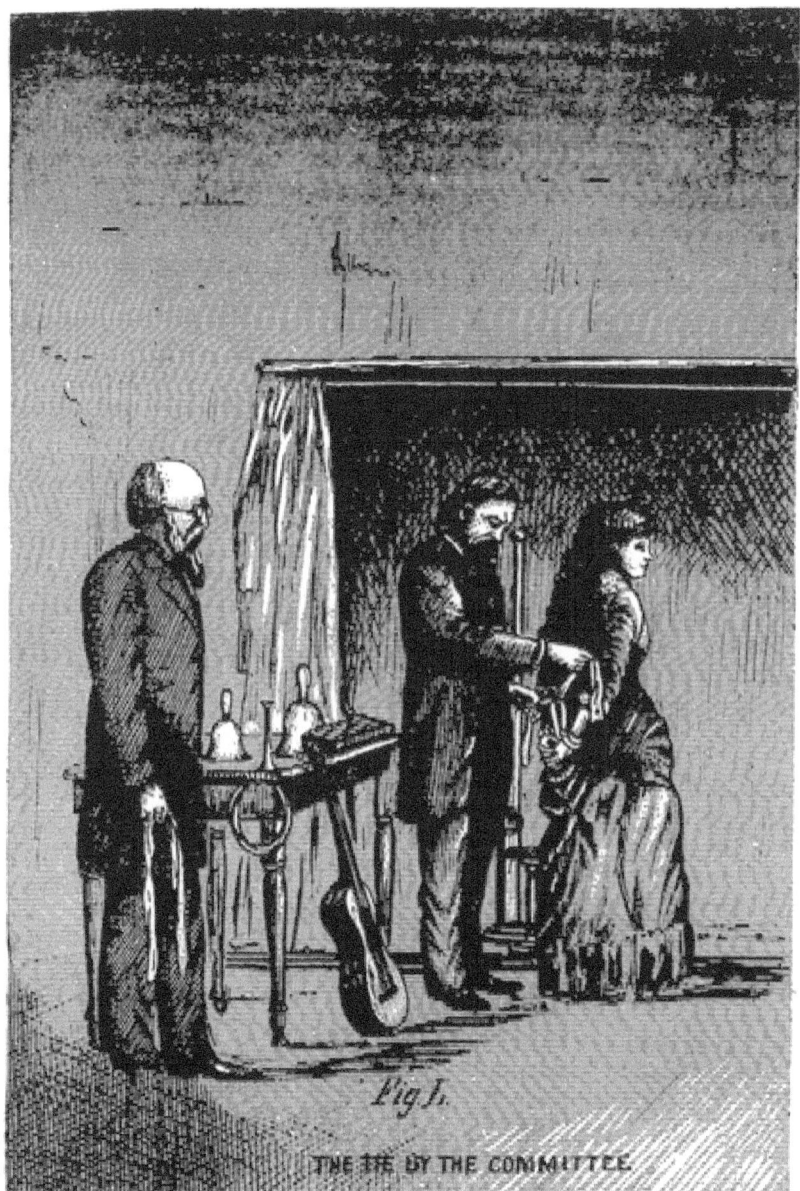

Fig. 1.

THE TIE BY THE COMMITTEE.

wrists. The great "Religious Illustrated Lecturer" now steps forward, and, in the most graceful manner imaginable, passes another cloth bandage about this ligature, in the centre of which he ties a plain double square knot, inviting both committee-men to tie several additional knots, which they do, as shown in Figure L, page 252. The medium is now seated upon a stool in the cabinet, facing the audience, with her back close to a wooden stanchion, about six feet high, which has been firmly fastened to the floor. The ends of the cotton bandage are now secured to a ring attached, by a staple, to the stanchion, at a point just above the stool upon which she is seated. A cotton bandage is then tied around the medium's neck, the ends of which are fastened to a screw-eye affixed to the stanchion, in order firmly to secure her head. Her feet are then fastened together by means of a cord, passing around the ankles, the long end of which is carried outside of the cabinet, to be held by one of the committee. The silver-tongued lecturer now gracefully places a tambourine, a tin horn and one or two bells on the medium's lap, and, suiting his words to the action, proceeds to "air his vocabulary," as follows: " Ladies and gentlemen: Your committee having securely tied the lady to the ring in the stanchion, with her hands fastened behind her in such a manner as to render them entirely helpless, having also bound her head, so that she cannot bend her body, while her feet are secured by this stout cord, the end of which is still guarded by your committee, I will close the curtain and hide her from your vision, for a little season, in order to ascertain if sufficient power has been generated to manifest through these musical instruments." The orator is here interrupted by a blow upon his head from the tambourine, which the spirits (or some unknown force) have ejected from the cabinet, through an aperture in the curtain. Bells are now rung, a horn is blown and general confusion reigns, until a strange, childish

THE COTTON-BANDAGE TEST. 255

voice calls out "Light!" which indicates the end of Act First.

On opening the cabinet, the medium does not appear to have moved in the least. The committee now step forward and carefully examine the knots, which they report as still intact, indicating that some occult force, outside the medium, must have created the demonstrations.

The Great Religious Lecturer now places a wooden hoop on the lady's lap, and, closing the curtain, continues: "The beauty of this little experiment consists in the remarkable rapidity of its execution." Here he is again interrupted by the ejaculation, "Light!" when the hoop is found resting upon her shoulders. A silk hat is then placed on her lap, which, when the curtain is drawn, appears upon the medium's head.

A tambourine, with a glass, partly filled with water, standing upon it, is now placed on the medium's lap, when the oily-tongued speaker continues as follows: "My friends:

We are about to try one of the most interesting and convincing experiments in spiritual phenomena that the world has ever witnessed. The physical manifestations exhibited thus far have been confined wholly to the movements of ponderable substances, which may possibly be acted upon by some occult force, other than spirit-power; but, now, we propose to demonstrate that there is intelligence connected with this force, and that it cannot be attributed to electricity, animal magnetism, psychology, or any other power heretofore suggested by scientists, ostensibly to disprove the integrity of the spirits, but really to conceal their own ignorance. When we were in London, England, a short time since, a committee, consisting of twelve of the most astute members of the Royal Æsthetical Association, were appointed to investigate the various phenomena attributed to our spirit friends, *solely in the interests of Science.* After a thorough canvass of the whole subject, occupying several months, during which we had the honor of entertaining them many times, giving all the assistance in our power to aid them in the solution of these mysteries, eleven of the members frankly acknowledged, in their report, in substance, that they could attribute the manifestations occurring in our presence to no other force than spirit-power. The twelfth member of the committee—a celebrated scholar—did not fully agree with his colleagues as to the cause of the phenomena. He fully acknowledged their existence, and confessed that it was not in the power of mere human agency to produce them, but he attributed all these physical manifestations to an inexplicable agency, something akin to electricity, which he called *odic* or *psychic* force. Now it is, doubtless, a fact well known to every member of this intelligent and discriminating audience, that glass is an absolute non-conductor of electricity—hence, the introduction of the forthcoming beautiful experiment. We have placed the glass of water on the medium's lap, while her head, hands and feet are firmly secured, rendering her, as you observe, entirely helpless; I will now close the curtain, and, should there be sufficient power in the control to induce the glass of water to rise to the lady's lips—allowing her to drink the contents—and, then, to replace the empty goblet in its original position, I think we shall have thoroughly exploded the theory of psychic, or odic, force." On opening the cabinet, the glass is found lying empty upon the medium's lap, as predicted by the orator, which marvel brings out a round of applause from the entire house. The committee now come forward and make a most thorough examination of the cotton-bandage tie, and duly report to the excited audience that the lady remains just as they had bound her, and that the phenomenon cannot properly be attributed to any human agency.

"Having thoroughly demonstrated the fact," continues the *suave* time-killer, "that these manifestations are not of an electric character, and that the medium is wholly unable to move her members during their occurrence, I now desire to further prove her entire honesty in this whole matter by allowing some elderly person to sit behind the curtain and hold the medium during the next experiment.

"The person thus favored must, however, allow me to blindfold him, as the force which manifests cannot withstand the power of the physical eye." ('That strain, again!' Shakspeare.) The question is often asked, by the skeptical world, why these exhibitions usually occur in the dark, or why, if they take place in the light, they are invariably cut off from our vision by some curtain or screen. In reply, I can only repeat, what I have said a thousand times before, that I do not know. I only know that these are among the imperative conditions exacted by our spirit-friends in order that they may be enabled to manifest. If you would all voluntarily close your eyes, as the medium does, during the occurrence of the phenomena, there would be no necessity for a screen; but, among a multitudinous assemblage, like the one before me, there are doubtless many persons of a temperament so nervous, that they would involuntarily open their eyes during the manifestations, which would be fatal to the medium. In order, therefore, to prevent the possibility of such an occurrence, I am obliged to cut off the human vision, in the manner suggested. It is claimed, by our most advanced thinkers, that there is a power in the physical eye which wholly neutralizes the force of the spirit, when acting upon visible things—just as one chemical will destroy another, just as water will quench fire; but *why* these facts exist is a problem too deep for me to solve. I place it with the rest of the things which are inscrutable, and leave it there."

The blindfolded and credulous investigator is now placed within the cabinet, with his right hand upon the medium's lap, while his left rests upon his head, as shown in Figure M, page 260.

The instant the curtain is closed, spirit voices, mingled with discordant strains of music, are plainly heard; a bell faintly jingles;

Fig. M.

THE HOLDING TEST.

a hoop passes over the investigator's head; the animated guitar seems to float about within the cabinet, as if some living human being really controlled its movements, while the medium, so far as the investigator is aware, remains rigid and motionless.

At the conclusion of this experiment, the investigator leaves the cabinet, and an infinite variety of similar spiritual phenomena follow. An empty pail passes, unseen, from the medium's lap to an inverted position upon her head. A tambourine flies out of the cabinet at the aperture, to the amazement of all beholders. A finger-ring is mysteriously transferred from the medium's lap to the tip of her nose. Paper dolls are cut by the same invisible agency. A nail is driven into a board by some spirit-carpenter, who makes as much noise as if he were still in the flesh. Names of deceased townsmen, with dates of birth and death, are frequently written behind the curtain, upon a slate in the medium's lap, a fact which clearly indicates to the most skeptical that there is an alert intelligence connected with this occult force. It is a remarkable fact, in this connection, that the accuracy of these names and dates can be easily confirmed by a visit to the nearest cemetery, or a close perusal of the obituary notices contained in the files of local newspapers! This part of the wonderful entertainment is concluded by the spirits, who cut the medium loose, at the request of the orator of the evening, in such a manner as to leave the knots at the wrists intact, including the sewing. The knots are now triumphantly exhibited to the electrified audience, and the "Indescribable Phenomenon" leaves the stage amid deafening shouts of applause.

Henry Melville Cummings Fay Foster Mansfield Braddon now enters the cabinet, carrying—in addition to all his names—a long cotton cord in his hand, when the curtain is closed and his alleged control, "War Eagle," the spirit of a defunct and rampant Indian chief, proceeds to tie him with the "great front-twist," generally regarded as the most intricate and inextricable knot imaginable. At a signal from within, the cabinet is opened, when Fay is presented to the audience lashed to his chair, with both hands tied to his knees, in an apparently immovable position. See Figure X, page 264. The committee make a hasty examination of all the knots, and report the medium to be securely bound, so that neither hand can be removed, without untying the whole rope—a fact which it certainly seems impossible for the medium to accomplish, as the final knots at the ends of the rope are fastened to the lower rounds of his chair, entirely beyond his reach. Another chair is now placed at his right side, upon which are several large, solid iron rings, which have been previously circulated among the audience for inspection. The spiritual Demosthenes now begins to harangue his hearers something as follows: " The spirits in control are about to introduce one of the most convincing evidences of their power ever witnessed in any public or private seance. Unlike most of the spiritual manifest-

264 THE COTTON-BANDAGE TEST.

Fig. X.

ations occuring in our presence, we are able to name and describe this phenomenon in advance. It is called the 'Lyman Test,' so named after Professor Lyman, of Yale College, who introduced this experiment, some years ago, for the sole purpose of demonstrating to the skeptical world the power of our spirit-friends to accomplish apparent impossibilities. Before Professor Lyman's discovery, the incredulous scientists of all nations met our most astounding and miraculous spiritual feats with smiles of derision. It was a knock-down argument, with these *savants*, when they gravely informed our greatest mediums that *certain fixed laws of nature cannot be set aside, even by spirits*. But, thanks to Professor Lyman, these delusions are now happily dispelled, and we are able to boldly state to the world that, under proper conditions, *nothing is impossible when opposed by the full force of spiritual dynamics*.

"You will observe that my control has secured my physical form by an intricate network of ropes and knots, in such a manner

that your committee are fully satisfied
human power could release me in less
half an hour ; and, yet, the moment the cu
cuts off the magnetism of your gross phy
eyes, 'War Eagle,' my spirit control,
utterly dematerialize this chair, and diss
these solid iron rings into thin air, and
quickly rematerialize them all upon this phy
right arm." The curtain is now closed for a
seconds only, when the cabinet is again ope
and, lo! the great medium's words are
verified, as shown in Figure V, page 266.

An entertainment of this kind always d
ops, at least, one skeptical person among
audience, who is continually venting his
credulity in the form of smart suggesti
He is usually a sailor, or the captain of a ca
boat, who imagines that he "knows the rop
and who has more to say than the manage
either of the committee-men. This crotcl
individual is now invited to come upon
stage and untie the medium. The first
or three loose knots about the chair-leg

THE COTTON-BANDAGE TEST.

easily overcome; but it is not long before the task becomes more difficult. Fifteen or twenty minutes are usually spent in fruitless endeavors; small boys begin to hoot from the galleries; until at last, "smart man" grows red in the face, and, after a few more hopeless attempts, is compelled to abandon the contest, and retires amid peals of laughter from all parts of the house. The curtain is now closed, and, two minutes later, the medium steps out of the cabinet, free and unincumbered. A challenge is then offered to any man in the house to enter the cabinet and bind the medium, if possible, so that the spirits cannot untie him. This challenge usually brings upon the stage skeptic Number Two, who proceeds to tie the medium according to the best of his ability, when the curtain is again closed and the spirits at once release the medium in the manner described on page 234. A voice is now heard within the cabinet, asking the committee to release the medium, upon the ground that the power is diminishing and the conditions are growing unfavorable. Yells come from the gallery: "Keep him in there all night!" &c. The countenance of our skeptical friend beams with satisfaction, while he looks over the house with an air which plainly says, "I told you so; I've tied him, this time, so he'll stay put!"

At last, the audience become weary, and, at the suggestion of the committee, the self-satisfied manipulator generously volunteers to release his prisoner. He triumphantly draws back the curtain, when, to his utter amazement, no one is to be seen within! While, with a crest-fallen expression, he is engaged in inspecting the interior of the cabinet, Fay appears at the side of it, with the untied rope in his hand, and dismisses the audience amid tumults of applause.

The true inwardness of these demonstrations. —A Diakka now in control, who is friendly to the cause, having served an apprenticeship of over twenty-five years in spiritual matters, desires to attest the genuineness of these celebrated mediums, by explaining some of the foregoing phenomena—together with the accompanying illustrations, which those not versed in spiritual matters might possibly misinterpret. "It is a very common error," he impresses me to say, "among skeptical people, as well as some of our less pronounced spiritual friends, to hastily condemn as impostures the most remarkable spiritual manifestations, the moment they discover the methods by which the phenomena are made to occur.

Heretofore, it has not been thought advisable to make public the fact that the cotton-bandage test and the great front-twist are simply a blind, practiced by the spirits *solely for the good of the cause.* But to-day, we are stronger in the faith; our numbers having swelled to millions, we can bear more light, and, perhaps, use it to advantage. If deception has been practiced by the spirits, in their manifestations through the great front-twist and the cotton-bandage test, they have always created the delusion with the approbation of our staunchest members, and our most accomplished and reliable mediums, who justify their acts by pointing to the converts who so numerously follow. In short, the spirits seem to have allowed, in extreme cases, a little evil to be done that great good might be accomplished. No medium with an ounce of brains now believes, for a moment, that the spirits can instantly disintegrate and reunite solid iron rings upon a man's arm, without heat or chemical action. Such an extraordinary feat can only be accomplished by them at the Royal Mechanical Laboratory of Spiritual Science, which lies way beyond the Great Draco Major Belt, and through which none of our Diakka band can, at present, penetrate. No medium of ordinary intelligence believes that the spirits can elevate a water-bucket from a woman's lap to the top of her head *except through the aid of some living physical, organism,* notwithstanding many mediums pretend to believe it, and continue to teach the doctrine,—*all for the good of the cause.* Very few persons of a high

THE GLASS OF WATER
Spirits Disproving the Agency of Electricity

order of intellect now believe that, away off in some remote corner of this universe, there exists a literal lake of everlastingly-burning brimstone—yet this theory has been proclaimed by religious teachers for ages, *solely for the good of the cause.* The Santa Claus story is charming — very fascinating to small children, who firmly believe that their behavior governs, in a degree, the quality and quantity of 'goodies' he will bring them on Christmas Eve; but children of a larger growth are supposed to have dismissed the delusion, to have discovered who Santa Claus really is, and just how he distributes his gifts. So it is hoped that the few remaining cranky children in our ranks, who are still afraid of the true science and *art* of spirit manifestations, will eventually outgrow their pet delusion, so long taught "for the good of the cause"—that spirits work apart from the medium, and not directly through him. When these mistaken ones become so far developed that they can bear just a few of the bright sun-rays of truth in regard to all spirit phenomena termed physical demonstrations, then, and not till then, will the cause make rapid and triumphant strides. The accompanying cuts must reveal to every observer the fact that our spirit-friends manifest wholly through their medium, in the cotton-bandage tie; a fact which can be further substantiated by a little calculation and explanation. By the peculiar manner in which the medium holds her hands, while submitting to the tying process on the part of the committee, as shown in Figure J, page 272, the spirits secure, for their uses, a ligature of knotted cloth between the hands, at least six inches in length. The bandage attached to the centre, as before mentioned, is usually tied in four or five double square knots, allowing, at least, two inches' play between the centre of the ligature and the ring to which it is fastened. This ring is two and a half inches in diameter, and is secured to the stanchion by a half-inch staple. The medium's left hand adds six inches more, while the bandage on her wrist will easily

Fig K.

GENERAL MANIFESTATIONS, THROUGH THE COTTON BANDAGE TIE

slip along her slender and delicate arm, at least half way to the elbow—all which gives the spirits a clear leeway of not less than twenty inches from the stanchion. The moment the curtain is closed, the medium, under spirit influence, spreads her hands as far apart as possible, an act which stretches the knotted ligature so that the bandage about it will easily slip from the centre to either wrist ; then, throwing her lithe form, by a quick movement, to the left, so that her hips will pass the stanchion, without moving her feet from the floor, the spirits are able, through the medium, to reach whatever may have been placed upon her lap.

During the holding test, no such contortions of her body are necessary, as the ubiquitous manager always takes good care to place the neck of the guitar close to the medium's hands, as shown in Figure M, page 260.

In the Lyman test, illustrated by Figure W, page 307, the spirits employ the great front-twist. Through their influence, the medium's left wrist is made fast at his knees, as in loop

274 THE COTTON-BANDAGE TEST.

5. Figure F, below, by permanent knot 1. The right hand is then inserted in the open

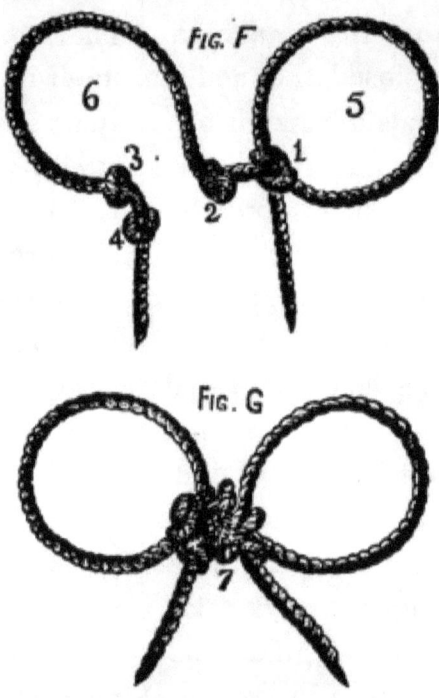

loop 6, and, by twisting it once around, allowing the rope to roll on the wrist, the space between knots 3 and 4 cross 1 and 2, forming the complete and intricate knot 7, shown in

Fig. N.
THE HOLDING TEST DURING MANIFESTATIONS

Figure G, page 274. When the curtain is closed, the right hand can be easily taken out of this tie, and replaced in an instant, as shown in Figure W, page 307. And these are the BOTTOM FACTS regarding the Great front-twist and the Cotton-bandage tie.

CHAPTER XXI.

So-called Exposures.

AMONG all the great mediums who have suffered persecution on account of what is commonly termed "Spiritual Exposures," probably no one is more conspicuous than that celebrated medium, Doctor Henry Slade. Hardly a twelvemonth has elapsed, during the last twenty years, in which some reporter, or amateur spirit-hunter, has not, Quixote-like, claimed to have detected Slade in fraudulent manifestations, and proceeded to declare him a miserable mountebank and a villainous trickster.

Fully nine-tenths of these sensational reports, I am inclined to believe, are the direct result of a misapprehension, on the part of the would-be exposers, as to what constitutes genuine spirit phenomena.

When Doctor Slade was in London, England, in 1876, on his way, as reported, to fill an engagement at St. Petersburgh, he gave several very successful seances to distinguished persons, including a few members of the Royal Society. Nothing occurred to hinder his progress in making converts to the glorious cause, until Professor Lankester, of the British Association for the Advancement of Science, while holding a circle with the Doctor, snatched the slate from its position under the corner of the table at the precise moment when the spirits, through the Doctor, began to make the sound which so closely imitates that of slate-writing —when, lo! it was found that the slate had already been written upon.

This fact alone was sufficient evidence to Professor Lankester, and his friend Doctor Donkin, who was also present, that Slade was no true medium, but rather a bungling juggler. It is plainly evident from Professor Lankester's letters to the London *Times*, describing his experience with Slade, that he expected the spirits were to manifest directly upon inanimate matter; that an invisible spiritual power was prepared to create an invisible physical structure, or body—but without animal life—and that, through the body so created, a bit of pencil was, in some manner, to be seized by the spirit and moved about upon the surface of a slate with sufficient force to cause a part of the material of the pencil to adhere to its surface—thereby leaving a communication conveying intelligence appreciable by his gross physical senses.

Thus it was that this great medium was frustrated in his good work; was subjected to the inconvenience of a trial, the expense of an attempted defence, the mortification of a conviction and imprisonment for vagrancy, wholly on account of the lamentable ignorance of Professor Lankester, the arrogant and unreasonable investigator.

SO-CALLED EXPOSURES. 279

Had Lankester been in possession of one simple fact known to every prominent medium in the world—that a spirit has no power to manifest to those in the physical form except through some living human organism—the whole of Doctor Slade's trouble in England would, in all probability, have been avoided. But ignorance brings its own cure. Perhaps this act of persecution was specifically ordained, in order that the truth might eventually be made known to the masses.

After Doctor Slade's arrest, he evidently fell into the hands of a band of unfriendly Diakka, who had decided in advance upon his conviction; for, yielding to their untoward influence, his first move was to injure his own case, almost irreparably, by deceiving his counsel.

Then, as if to add fuel to the fire of public indignation, he was induced to reply to Professor Lankester's letter, through the *Times*, as follows:

"Sir,—It very seldom occurs that I feel called upon to write in my own defence. To the statements of Professor Lankester, which appeared in the *Times* of the 16th instant, I think I may with propriety reply.

"These are the facts:—On our sitting down to the table, I held the slate against the under side of the table when, after some delay, the sound of the pencil writing on the slate was heard. On withdrawing the slate, there was found to be what might have been intended for a name, very poorly written upon the upper surface. I then wiped this off the slate, saying, 'I will hold it again; perhaps they will write plainer,' Again a little delay ensued, when I said to Professor Lankester, 'Perhaps if you take hold of the slate with me they will be better able to write.' He thereupon released his hand from where it was joined with my left, and those of his friend upon the table, and, instead of holding the slate with me, seized it, as he describes.

"Instead of there being a message written,

as he says, there were only two, or, at most, three, words on the upper surface of the slate.

"Now, had Professor Lankester listened as closely as he says he watched me, he must have heard me say, after asking him to hold the slate with me, 'They are writing now.' This was said while he was in the act of removing his hand from where it was joined on the table to the slate, for I heard the sound of the pencil when the writing commenced, while I was asking him to hold the slate with me. Consequently, when he seized the slate, only two or three words were found written upon it.

"Had he told me he suspected I was doing the writing, I think there would have been no difficulty in disabusing his mind on that point.

"That I do the writing with a piece of pencil under my finger-nail is an old theory. However, I always keep my nails so closely cut as to render that impossible, to which those who have taken the trouble to examine them can testify. Therefore, all I have to say is, I did not do the writing at the sitting with Professor Lankester, nor at any other sitting

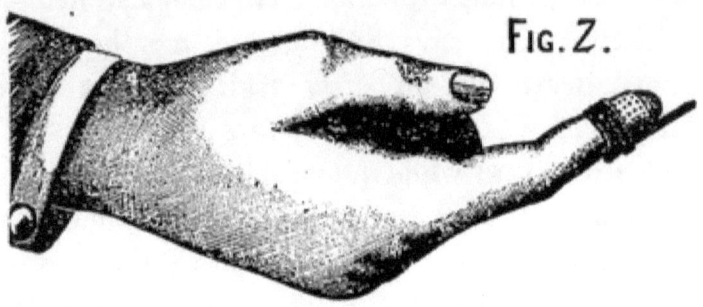

Fig. Z.

given by me during the years I have been before the public as a medium.

"Very truly yours,

"Henry Slade."

I herewith present another so-called exposure of the medium Slade, in consequence of which he experienced no little trouble, and likewise suffered considerable damage, through the unwise management of his friends. The account is taken from the Belleville, Ontario, *Daily Intelligencer*, and is as follows:

"The best-known of the slate-writing mediums, and the one generally acknowledged to be possessed of the greatest mediumistic power, is Dr. Henry Slade, of New York. His fame as a medium is world-wide, and he has confounded some of the most eminent thinkers in England, Germany, and Russia, as well as in America, by the wonderful phenomena which are produced by him. Knowing this, a number of gentlemen of this city, having heard much, read some, but seen but little of so-called spirit phenomena, determined to engage Dr. Slade for one week, to give daily sittings or seances. The arrangements were completed, the engagement was made, and Dr. Slade arrived in Belleville on Friday evening, the 30th ult., and put up at the Defoe House, where rooms had been engaged for him. The doctor's suave, gentlemanly manner, and apparently honest and sincere desire to work in the great cause to which he had devoted his life, created in many minds quite an impression in his favor. 'It does not matter,' he said earnestly to the writer, 'if only one person in Belleville is convinced of the fact of a future existence who was not convinced of it before, I will consider myself well repaid.'

"Such a noble illustration of disinterestedness and zeal could not but impress one with his honesty of purpose, notwithstanding the fact that he was to receive $150 and his expenses for the visit. Dr. Slade's sittings began, and the phenomena which were produced were certainly, at first, startling; but, after the first surprise, several of those who held successive sittings with him began to observe suspicious movements on the part of the doctor, not so much in the slate-writing (which, in most minds, remained a mystery up to the last, and is not satisfactorily explained to some even yet), as in the other phenomena with which the slate-writing was supplemented. These other phenomena were mere tricks, whether judged as spiritual manifestations or sleight-of-hand performances. The slate was passed under the table by some invisible agency into the hand of one of the sitters while both the doctor's hands were on the table; those sitting around the table had their limbs tapped and pressed, as by a hand, and occasionally their chairs were sharply jerked; a long pencil would be placed on a slate, and when the doctor would place the slate under the table the pencil would fly suddenly from under the table on to it, or over the heads of the sitters; if the 'amospheric conditions' were favorable, a large chair, which was always placed at a convenient distance from the doctor's chair, would suddenly fly toward him; and of course the raps under the table and in the vicinity of the medium were of frequent occurrence. In every one of these 'manifestations' the doctor was detected by different parties at different times. Sunday night, Mr. James Starling distinctly saw him throw the long pencil, with his thumb and finger, from the edge of the table over the heads of the company. He was also detected afterward by Mr. J. Northcott and others. This is a simple trick, and can be done by any one with a little practice. Dr. Abbott, in the course of his only sitting, looked suddenly under the table while loud raps were in progress and distinctly saw Slade's heel knocking against the rung of his chair. The raps under the table were of course produced by the toe of Slade's left slipper. The pressures and taps were undoubtedly produced by him. One who had sat with him two or three times and closely observed him could not fail to perceive that just before the taps and pressures would be made on the limbs of any one of the sitters, he would always pretend to be touched himself, and would shiver, jerk back his chair, and look under the table, giving a reason that he was so nervous that he did it instinctively. For his keen and practiced eye, just the one glance was sufficient to enable him to 'take in' the disposition of the legs of the company, and he could, with that snake-like left leg of his (which he always kept under the table, allowing the other to remain in full view of the company), touch any of the sitters wherever he pleased, with an unerring precision, so long as they kept their limbs in the same position. A close and suspicious observer could easily perceive this by the movement of Slade's body when he was manipulating his left leg. On one occasion, Mr. James Starling, who sat at the doctor's left, was touched on the left knee. He suddenly and very vigorously raised his right foot, and it came in contact with a material substance suspiciously resembling the calf of a leg, and the ownership of the said leg was immediately confirmed by an expression of pain on Slade's open countenance, and an uneasy start from that individual. After this 'manifestation' Slade objected to having Mr. Starling sit in the circle, on the ground that he had already sat five times, which, he claimed, should have satisfied him. On another occasion, after the party sitting opposite Slade had been touched several times on both limbs, the writer, who was sitting at Slade's left, suddenly crossed his legs immediately in front of the medium, so that that individual could not, by any possibility, get his foot beyond them without touching, not knowing them to be in that position. In a moment, there was a very palpable touch, not to say a kick, on the writer's left ankle, and Slade immediately afterward looked under the table.

"It is significant that so long as the writer kept his legs crossed in front of Slade, the gentleman sitting opposite Slade was not touched, though the party to his right was. As to the passing of the slate under the table, that was done with Slade's useful left foot, which he could bend forward so far that the toe almost touched the front of his leg. The slate rested flat on the sole of his slipper, and in this manner he passed it along to any one in the circle to whom 'the spirits' were directed to send it. Mr. A. McGinnis, leaning back in his chair quietly, saw Slade's foot with the slate resting on it. Mr. W. Templeton also glanced under the table hastily on one occasion, but was observed by the doctor, and Mr. Templeton, though he did not see the slate on his foot, saw the slate fall to the floor and Slade's foot draw back like lightning to his chair. The spirits attempted four times to carry the slate to the writer, but failed each time, the slate falling to the ground before it could reach his hand. The reason given by Slade was that the writer held his hand beyond the magnetic current, and the spirits could not carry the slate past that current. The real reason was that, as soon as Slade announced that the slate had left his hand, the writer moved his hand about eighteen inches from the rim of the table, where he could see, if the slate reached his hand, whether it was conveyed by any visible power. (It is perhaps necessary to explain that during all these manifestations Slade insists that all in the circle must join hands in the middle of the table— thus making it necessary for them to come up close to the table.) On Thursday Chief McKinnon detected Slade twitching with his toe the chair of the man on his left, and another gentleman distinctly saw him, with his left leg, wheel an arm-chair that was standing a few feet away, up to the table.

Several other discoveries could be mentioned if we had space to enumerate them. But though the trick part of the phenomena was all made clear, the slate-writing remained a mystery. This much was clear, that it was not the work of spirits, for the writer received gushing messages from persons still living, whose names he had written on the slate. These yet embodied spirits wrote that they were present, were happy to be so, and one was so kind as to promise to remain always with the writer—in the capacity of office bore, it is to be presumed. There was no doubt in the majority of minds that the messages were fraudulent, but how they were produced was a puzzle. There was no doubt that when one of the circle wrote a name on the back of the slate and handed it to Slade, he contrived to read it while he held the slate under the table. As soon as the slate was well under the edge of the table, the spirits began to make his arm shake, and of course his wrist would shake and twist, and of course the slate, being in his hand, would shake and twist also, several times being turned completely over, so that he could read the name without any difficulty. Usually, however, he contented himself with allowing the slate to assume a perpendicular position, so that he could get a peep at the initials, without reading the whole name. As to how he produced the writing when the slate was under the table, no one could explain (and indeed it still remains unaccounted for). It may be observed, however, that no message in answer to a question was produced, while the slate was in that position, which was longer than a dozen words or so ; they were always written in a cramped, unnatural hand, which, often, no one but himself could read ; and they were written within a short space, not extending the full length and width of the slate, like the messages not in reply to questions, which were supposed to be written between enclosed slates. The writing produced between closed slates, or with the slate flat on the table, was, moreover, regularly and well written, and could be read with ease.

Several persons maintained that the writing between the closed slates was not produced at the time when it was supposed to occur, but that one of the slates which were placed together had writing on it when they were placed together, and that Slade deceived the sitters by sleight of hand when he pretended to show each side of both slates. Several persons had become convinced of this, but no one wished to be the party to snatch the slates and expose the trick. Chief McKinnon, however, at a seance on Wednesday, also became convinced, and decided to make a test. Accordingly, an arrangement was made by several parties to go together to the sitting yesterday morning at 10 o'clock, and the person on whose arm or shoulder Slade should rest the two closed slates was to grasp them and wrest them from him as soon as the writing should commence. Those who were present at that sitting were Chief McKinnon, E. McMahon, and Alderman Dickson.

When the time for the closed-slate feat

came, Slade reached his hand, as usual, to the little stand behind him that held his slates, selected a slate, and appeared to show both sides of it, as well as those of the one on the table. He closed them together, as usual, with a scrap of pencil between them, and held them on McMahon's shoulder. In a moment the scratching began. But it was not heard longer than two seconds, when Mr. McMahon suddenly seized the slates, wrested them from Slade, and laid their inner surfaces open on the table. One of the slates was entirely covered with writing which, on examination, proved to be the following, which is but a specimen of all the platitudes that have been supposed to come from the spirit-land through Slade's mediumship, and which is given exactly as written, even to punctuation :

"You are all the children of the infinit; your times are the measure of endless years ; your labors are the search from immemorial wisdom ; your destiny is the joy and love—now it is time you all began to realize this fact and prepare to meet the change from earth to spirit; you cannot prepare unless you look more to the laws of spirit and of God—this is all I shall say now. God bless you all."

Slade, with the evidence of his fraud confronting him, did not make any attempt at explanation. He wilted at once, and appeared for a time quite dazed and stupid. But when Chief McKinnon threatened to arrest him for fraud, he begged with tears and sobs to be allowed to leave town. He acknowledged that all the phenomena which had taken place were fraudulent, and that Spiritualism had nothing whatever to do with them. He offered to show how he produced the trick which had just been exposed, and explained it in this way: When he took the slate from the stand behind him it contained the message just quoted, which he had written while he was alone, before the sitting began. By sleight-of-hand manipulation, which is very easily understood when seen, he made it appear that he wiped and showed the two sides of each slate, while the fact is that he had wiped and showed only one side of the one that had the writing on. The scratching noise was produced by his finger, and the final tap on the slate denoting that the message is complete, by the same means. When told that he would probably be arrested, he paced the floor in extreme trepidation, and entreated piteously to be allowed to leave the city at once, declaring that if arrested he would certainly cut his throat. Steps were taken to procure his arrest, but after the information had been laid, and while the warrant for his arrest was being made out, two or three of those who had been most active in unearthing his deceptions, moved to pity by his entreaties, his tears and promises, pleaded for him and secured him his liberty. He left by the noon train for the east. Before he left the city he attempted to do something to retrieve himself. To one gentleman he said that when he admitted that his manifestations were the results of trickery he told a lie in order to avoid arrest, and was ready, on account of fear, to admit or deny anything. He told the cabman who drove him to the station that a certain gentleman who had prominently interested himself in the recent affair had got him drunk, and that he (Slade) was not responsible for what he had done or said.

Since he has gone, there are several persons who have had repeated sittings with him who are not satisfied with the explanation he gave of the production of writing within the closed slates. They say that they know the writing could not have occurred in that way, because they brought their own marked slates to the sittings, had examined them closely on both sides before the writing came, and that Slade had never attempted to substitute any other slates in place of those they brought. However that may be, there is no doubt whatever that the manifestations which take place at night in Slade's bedroom are produced by himself. This was demonstrated on Thursday night to the complete satisfaction of the writer, who shared Slade's bed with him for some time that night. About a quarter of an hour after the writer turned off the gas and got into bed, loud raps came apparently from the back of the bed near the writer's head. Slade immediately began to tremble and cower down in the bed, and in reply to the question what was the matter with him, he said the spirits were there and were going to do something, for he was being touched all over. The rapping continued, now at the head of the bed, now at the foot, now apparently under it—Slade never ceasing to shake and press close to his bed-fellow and clutch him by the arms convulsively. After this interesting performance had lasted for about ten minutes, Slade asked the writer to address the spirits and ask them whether there would be manifestations during the night; he said himself that he thought it was rather late for them to manifest with much power. (It was then after 2 A. M.) The writer said aloud, 'Well, do you intend to produce any manifestations to-night?' Three loud raps, signifying 'yes,' was the reply. Suddenly Slade rose on his left elbow and extended his right arm over the speaker's breast. 'Look,' he said, 'at that bright light just at the foot of the bed. Oh, look! don't you see it, just in the direction that I am pointing?' He continued in this way for about a minute, directing attention to a supposed light in the room, which, to the writer's unspiritual eyes, remained vailed in Egyptian darkness. Slade then pointed in the direction of the bedroom door, shooting out his long, lithe arm suddenly over the writer's breast, and directing his attention to a most brilliant violet light in that direction. He was informed that his energetic pointing was rather unnecessary, for in the darkness his hand could not be seen, and he was civilly requested to be quiet. He paid no attention to the request, however, but, almost immediately after it was made, threw himself with considerable force against the writer, and stretched his arm far over his body. Something was heard to clank against the side of the bed, and the passive occupant of the bed knew almost as well as its active occupant that something was coming. He was not disappointed. In four or five seconds something decidedly hard and heavy fell, as if from the ceiling, on his bare shin, which lay outside the covers in case of an emergency. He leaned forward and clutched the object, and, feeling it, discovered it to be a smooth walking-stick with a metal knob. He quietly placed one end on the floor and held on to it with his right hand, 'What was that thing that fell on the bed?' asked Slade, after a moment's pause. 'Only a bit of a stick,' was the reply.

A few minutes afterward, Slade began groping with his left hand to find out what had become of the stick. He found his companion's right arm hanging by the side of the bed, and he asked, presently, 'Have you my *walking stick* in your hand?' The fellow had no doubt concealed the stick somewhere near the head of the bed when he retired, in case any 'manifestations' would be required. The writer then caught Slade's both hands in his left hand and held them close to his breast, and demanded that the manifestations should continue under those conditions. Slade protested against this, and alternately argued, whimpered and threatened, but he finally submitted. After a short time, the writer was touched on the right leg several times and the rappings were renewed around the bed. After lying passive for a minute or two, the writer raised his left leg as quickly as he could; it came in contact with Slade's left leg, which was evidently performing gyrations in the air. The first-mentioned leg rose higher than the other, and came down on it, pinning both of Slade's legs to the bed. Then grasping Slade's wrists tightly, the writer requested that the manifestations be continued. Slade writhed a little, protested much, and again threatened and whined, but again submitted, with very little resistance —strangely enough, for he is very powerful in the upper part of the body. For ten or fifteen minutes the two remained in that position, and during that time there was not the faintest suspicion of a manifestation—not a rap, not a touch, nothing. Finally a cramp in the left leg brought on by keeping it so long in a strained position, induced the writer to release Slade. He then rose, dressed himself, and left the great medium to his dreams—not, however, without first denouncing him as a fraud.

Before closing, we wish to say a word about the character of this individual, apart from his profession of medium-juggler-swindler, and we hope that this article will be copied into newspapers throughout Canada and the States, so that society may be warned against him, and he may be driven into private life. It is impossible to enter here into a minute description of Slade, but he is most assuredly a creature not fit for the companionship of respectable people." . . . .

Shortly after the foregoing attempted exposure appeared in print, the *Banner of Light* unfortunately inflicted another serious blow upon the cause, by categorically denying that the medium operating in Belleville was the original Doctor Henry Slade.

Acting upon the illogical supposition that the wrath of his enemies must be appeased by the sacrifice of some one, the *Banner* virtually characterized the genuine manifestations referred to as fraudulent, laying the whole blame upon the shoulders of another medium, as the following article from its columns will show:

"Information reaches us from Montreal, Canada, that an individual who goes about that country calling himself—or by inference agreeing to allow others to call him—'Dr. Slade,' is now operating in that part of the continent, and has just been exposed in Belleville, Ont. We are glad to hear that to such an extent, at least, justice has overtaken him. We would inform our readers in Montreal, Belleville, and elsewhere, that Dr. (Henry) Slade, of New York city, the genuine proprietor of the name, is at present lecturing in Michigan, and is not, nor has he been of late, in Canada. The person claiming his name and reputation is either the party who is known as 'Charles Slade,' against whom we have repeatedly warned our patrons, or else some one of the Braddon-Fay-*et-al* combination now imposing upon the Canadian people has assumed the name of Slade to escape the effects of the showing up which we gave these 'worthies' in our issue of June 3d. The New York *Sun* paragraphs this 'Belleville' business as applying to the genuine Dr. Slade, but its attempt to injure a worthy medium is beneath contempt, and is too absurd to need an answer."

Abundant proof is at hand to show that the medium referred to by the Belleville Intelligencer *was* the genuine Doctor Henry Slade. Not the least among the evidences of this fact is the following letter, which appeared in the New York *Truth Seeker*, November 29, 1882 :

BELLEVILLE, July 19, 1882.

"TO THE EDITOR OF THE TRUTH SEEKER:

Sir: I have just received your letter, and noted its contents. As to it not being the genuine Dr. Henry Slade, who was so completely exposed here, I can and will prove that it was, also that the people in the *Banner of Light* office are mistaken. Here are the proofs:

First. The first letter we sent reached Slade through the *Banner of Light* office.

Second. Slade was recognized by Mr. H. Tammadge, of this city, as the same man who was on trial in London several years ago.

Third. He was recognized by Mr. C. J. Starling, who visited him several times in New York city.

Fourth. He was recognized both from photographs and engravings in illustrated papers, in possession of several of us here.

Fifth. In a letter written to a gentleman of this city, Mr. F. H. Rous, written after the exposure, he attempts to excuse himself. I send you the paper, so you can judge with what success.

Sixth. While here, many letters were received by him, all addressed to Dr. Henry Slade, and several were forwarded from the *Banner of Light*.

There are several other proofs, among which are the improbability of an impostor wearing several thousand dollars' worth of diamonds and having several hundred dollars with him, as this man had. You can tell the *Banner of Light* people that if he was a bogus Slade they should send us the money we are out, as it was their fault, they giving the bogus our letter instead of the genuine. But it was certainly the genuine humbug, and if they still deny it we will send a committee to New York and unmask him as thoroughly as we did here. If there is a genuine medium, they ought to send him to Belleville, but they won't. 'Fraud will not stand honest investigation; truth courts it.'

The reason Slade was allowed to escape is,

he was a member of the Masonic body, so were some of his captors; also, it is likely he made a liberal use of his ill-gotten gains to grease their palms.   Yours truly,

Joseph Templeton."

In the present undeveloped condition of the masses concerning spiritual things, it may well be expected that the secular press, out of sheer ignorance of the laws governing spiritual manifestations, will embrace every possible opportunity to defame and injure the cause, by cool attempts to expose the choicest and most prominent mediums. But when a leading spiritual paper, like the *Banner of Light*, which almost wholly lives and thrives upon the spiritualists themselves, consents to kill the goose which lays its golden eggs, by indulging in disreputable and unwarrantable attacks upon such a distinguished medium as Doctor Charles Slade, it is proper to look for the reason of the strange proceeding.

It has been my good fortune to hold a

number of very satisfactory sittings with this much-abused medium, and, although he is quite ready to acknowledge his inferiority to Henry Slade, in a particular phase of manifestations, it must, at the same time, be admitted by all the candid, that, in connection with other phases, he is vastly superior to the medium whose patronymic he bears. From a personal acquaintance with both these gentlemen, I feel justified in classing them together among the few great champions and exponents of the spiritual system. There is no sort of propriety in praising the one and decrying the other.

If the paper above named intends to brand mediums as tricksters and impostors as fast as they discover some new fragment of the true laws which govern all spiritual manifestations, the hour will speedily arrive when *all* mediums must be placed in one and the same category, and then what will become of the *Banner of Light?*

CHAPTER XXII.

TO SPIRITUAL MEDIUMS ONLY.

[CONFIDENTIAL.—The author trusts to the honor of all readers —except Spiritual Mediums—that they will omit this chapter.]

DIAKKA, under whose partial control I now find myself, and who claims to have influenced hundreds of our best mediums, during the last twenty-five years, in the exhibition of almost every phase of spirit phenomena, desires to give amateur mediums the benefit of his vast and fruitful experience—believing that all such persons may become experts in the spirit business through a thorough understanding of the facts he is about to disclose. This Diakka does not subscribe to the opinion advanced in the foregoing pages—that the world is now prepared for the "BOTTOM FACTS" in all spirit manifesta-

tions. On the contrary, he believes that the "good of the cause" demands a continuation, for all time to come, of the established system of deception practiced by all mediums. He declares that *spiritual mediums can only retain their present power by keeping the masses in ignorance;* that universal knowledge of the mysteries of mediumship would soon destroy the whole fabric of Spiritualism ; that, at the moment when every man becomes his own medium, the cause must waste and perish, as surely as an army would be shorn of its power should every common soldier suddenly become a commissioned officer. In simple justice, therefore, to both sides in this grave controversy, I will yield myself to the influence, and allow this Diakka full control of my pen, on condition, however, that he alone be held responsible for whatever he may induce me to record. The Diakka says :

Among the fundamental and inevitable requirements of a first-class medium are an unlimited assurance, a talent for subtlety, absolute dexterity, and an easy conscience. Armed with these qualities, and furnished with a reasonable knowledge of the laws which govern spiritual things, no medium need ever fail.

If you desire to become a professional medium, leave home at once, for "A prophet is not without honor save in his own country and in his own house!" Strangers will frequently credit a man with that which his friends will be quick to deny him.

The most feasible way of introducing yourself to a new town, is by means of a systematic canvass of the same, with the ostensible purpose of disposing of some manner of merchandise,—such as books, patent-medicines and household utensils. Do not disclose to any one your real business, or your ultimate design. Keep your eyes and ears open, and learn all you possibly can, both of the living and the dead, among prominent spiritualists. Provide yourself with a blank-book suitable for the pocket, which contains an index. Under the proper letter, record every name and date

TO SPIRITUAL MEDIUMS ONLY. 311

which you imagine may be of future service. From these notes, you will be able to prepare, at your leisure, such a history as will materially assist you afterward. By the exercise of a little shrewdness, you can soon learn, at the post-office and principal news-rooms of the town, who are the greatest readers of spiritual papers, while the local cemetery will furnish you with desirable information concerning their friends who have passed into spirit life. With the names and dates thus secured, you will be able, in most instances, to make your brief histories more complete by referring to the obituary notices so plentifully to be found in the files of local newspapers.

This preliminary work is what is called by professional mediums "planting a town." The larger the area planted, and the more thorough the work, the more abundant the harvest. When you have carefully canvassed one town, according to these directions, proceed to another, and there repeat your labors. Never think of entering upon the harvest until you have planted, at least, six towns, although double the number would be still better. If, by any means, you can sustain yourself for a period sufficient to thoroughly plant from twelve to twenty large towns, a good business is virtually insured to you for life.

On returning to the town first planted, assume a sounding name, clothe yourself in the height of fashion, load yourself with suitable airs, register at the best hotel, and boldly announce your presence and the nature of your business to the most prominent spiritualists in the place. By no means despise the Press, but advertise liberally, announcing to the public that Professor Blank's—be sure and make it "Professor"—engagements are such that he can remain in the town but a very few days, hence those who would avail themselves of his marvelous powers must seize the first opportunity to confer with him.

One dollar per chair, at the regular circle, or five dollars for a private seance for one person, constitute the most popular prices among professional mediums. If you charge more, few people can afford to patronize you, while, if the terms are less, the masses will be very likely to characterize you as a novice, or condemn you as an impostor. Send complimentary cards of admission to a few of the wealthiest and most influential spiritualists of the place, whose names appear upon the record previously obtained by your planting system. These persons will be so astounded at the revelation, to you, of their identity, on the part of the spirits, that printed advertisements will not long be necessary—your patrons, themselves, will sound your praises everywhere.

The number of your first circle should not exceed half-a-dozen, and should consist mainly of elderly, or middle-aged, persons. It is well to delay the forming of the circle for some time after the arrival of the guests, in order to draw them into a general discussion of the subject of Spiritualism. This course invariably evokes certain unwitting remarks, which will materially assist the spirits in getting *en rapport* with the medium, as well as furnish him with valuable information. Always visit the cloak-room, and carefully inspect the pockets of all outer garments which you may find there, as well as the inside of every hat, for the benefit of the spirits and the "good of the cause"—to say nothing of the advantage which may accrue to yourself. When the circle is finally formed, seat yourself at one end of the table, with an elderly person on either side. When you begin to "see spirits," cause it to appear that their number is simply overpowering. Speak, at first, with great deliberation, and do not fail to make your descriptions quite general. Be very careful not to describe a spirit that is unduly tall or short, fat or lean, or in any way remarkable, until it has been recognized by some one who is friendly to the cause, and who, without knowing or intending it, will assist you to a more definite description. A dark-haired spirit is supposed to have dark eyes, while light hair and blue eyes are as likely to be conjoined in the spiritual world as in the material.

TO SPIRITUAL MEDIUMS ONLY.

All spiritual impressions should be described in a vague and almost inaudible manner, unless the spirit in control is working "planted" ground, where the medium is fully informed ; in which case, the clearer and more minute your descriptions the better. Never prostitute yourself, or the cause you serve, by stooping to personate a dead Indian, or the majority of the more intelligent spiritualists will promptly brand you as a fraud, and very properly withdraw from you altogether.

"The noble red man of the forest" has no love for civilization, even in its rudest form ; how, then, can it be expected that, in any case, or by any possibility, he can ascend to the sublime altitudes of spiritual science? When "Poor Lo" shuffles off his mortal coil, his freed spirit invariably seeks its affinities in "the happy hunting-grounds of the blest," from which, so far as our knowledge extends, he has never returned.

It is advisable to bring forward the ballot test—*a la* Charles Foster, at every circle, as this always adds to the mystery of the occasion and gives *eclat* to the performance.

If the history of the Widow Jones—who sits opposite—appears in your diary as a victim of planted territory, you may be quite sure that her ballot will contain the name of her deceased husband ; therefore, when she is called upon to write, you will not be obliged to change her ballot, or even to touch it, but may boldly invite the most skeptical person present to place the closed ballot on your forehead, when, as he pronounces the letters of the alphabet, you can correctly spell out the name. This piece of strategy will throw the skeptic completely off his guard, after which he will freely testify, with every other member of the circle, that you read *all* the ballots without taking them into your hands.

At the conclusion of each circle, carefully record the names of the persons composing it, together with those of the spirits that appeared, with the full particulars of their manifestations. These minutes, which prove so valuable to every medium for future reference, should be posted, in alphabetical order, in a ledger styled "The Harvest Record." Do not remain long in any town, during your initial trip, or first harvest, but so soon as the spiritualists attain to fever heat, in their excitement over your miraculous powers, abruptly take your leave and proceed to fill your next appointment. You will gain notoriety and popularity by the change, and, on your return to the same ground, your entertainments will be eagerly sought after, while your purse will show the amazing extent to which the appetite for spiritual wonders has been sharpened during your absence.

Never neglect an opportunity to gain information which will aid you in your professional venture. When you are invited out—as you are sure to be—to dine, or to pass an evening at a private house, always seek to draw your host, or hostess, into a discussion in the course of which you will be obliged to call for the family Bible, in order to prove some statement made, and, while looking for the required passage, carefully note the records of birth and death which are therein preserved. This will give you a *point*, and such points compose the chief stock-in-trade of every true medium. After you have gained confidence in your spirit control, through the ballot-test and others, it will answer to attempt the bolder experiment of slate-writing. This can be easily accomplished, with a very little practice, in the following manner: Purchase a book-slate, together with two small common slates, which are exact duplicates. Remove one of the leaves of the book-slate and cut it down to the exact size of the small ones. The pad thus furnished will be found to so closely resemble the surface of almost any slate that only the most critical examiner could distinguish the substitute from the original. Now write your spirit communication to some person whom you have reason to expect will be present at the circle you are about to hold. Conceal the writing by means of the pad, and put the slate in your inside coat-pocket, with the pad next your body, and you are fully equipped for business. The first experiment should be made with a small circle, composed entirely of spiritualists, so that, in case of accident or failure, you will be in the hands of your friends, who, notwithstanding your misfortune, will still give you their countenance and support. Remember that our shoulders are broad. We will be responsible for all your short-comings. You have full liberty to charge every imperfection to the Diakka, who were created expressly for your protection, "all for the good of the cause."

When the circle is formed, lay the clean slate upon the table, and be sure to call the attention of every one present to the fact that no writing appears upon it. As soon as all are satisfied upon this point, suggest a trifling change in the relative positions of those forming the circle, and, as some old lady takes her seat on the opposite side of the table, as directed by you, politely rise to assist her, and, at the same time, carelessly remove the clean slate from the table and place it under your arm. You will easily be able to exchange it for the one concealed in your pocket, as you stoop to perform this very natural act of courtesy to your aged guest.

Now resume your seat, and, after exhibiting both sides of the duplicate slate in a dim light, address the circle in some such terms as these: "Friends: It is claimed by our cold, materialistic antagonists, that more or less deception is invariably practiced in connection with slate-writing; that, in some inexplicable manner, the clean slate is exchanged, before your very eyes, for one upon which a message has already been written. Now, to disprove a theory so ridiculous, I propose to request this old gentleman upon my right, in whom you all repose the utmost confidence, to write his name upon the upper surface of this clean slate which I hold in my hand, in order that he may be able fully to identify it, should our spirit friends generate power enough to communicate."

The old gentleman will, of course, write his name upon the upper surface of the slate, as directed, while the under surface thereof, which appears to be clean, really bears the message already written, covered, of course, by the pad. Now put the slate under the leaf of the table and cautiously allow the pad to drop into your lap, then quickly turn the slate over, to bring the message upward. The party to whom the message is written should now be invited to take a seat at your right and to hold the slate firmly against the table-leaf with his left hand. Let some bits of pencil now be placed upon the upper surface of the slate, when, with a small piece hidden under your finger-nail, or by means of an open-top thimble, worn upon the first finger, to which is fastened a short pencil, as shown in Figure Z., page 281, you will be able, without being detected, to produce a scratching noise on the under side of the slate, which will imitate the sound of writing to perfection. At the conclusion of the pretended writing, a convulsive shudder—common to all mediums, and always effectual—should pass over your whole system, during which you can easily dispose of the thimble, especially as your victim is busily engaged in reading to the mystified circle his marvelous communication direct from the spirit-world.

There are numerous other methods of spiritual slate-writing, many of which, by the exercise of a little ingenuity, the average medium will be able to discover, and, by proper practice, to master. One of the most essential requirements of every medium, in this direction, is the art of inverted writing, which can only be acquired by careful study and long habit. Every medium will be occasionally called upon to sit for slate-writing without having previously prepared a message, and even without the essential aid of his own "magnetized" slate. In such cases, he is compelled to write upon the under side of a slate held beneath a table-leaf, as shown in Figure S. page 149. Unless he is an expert, and can readily write backwards, the message thus recorded will, when the slate is turned over, appear reversed, a fact which will be sure to subject him to the charge of imposture. If, on the contrary, the message is written in reverse, so that, when the slate is turned over, it will appear to be correctly executed, the most skeptical person—if unacquainted with this method—will be led to believe that the writing was done upon the upper surface of the slate, and, consequently, must, in his judgment, have been performed by a spirit, or some occult force, and not by the medium. No slate-writing medium who can write in reverse need ever be caught napping. All the paraphernalia he will require are the pencil-thimble and the pencil-clamp, which can always be carried about his person, and should be deposited in the handkerchief-pocket. See illustrations Y. and Z., pages 199, 281.

With these simple devices, together with a reasonable amount of practice, the medium will be prepared successfully to write upon any slate whatsoever, by strictly observing the following simple directions:

After carefully washing a slate upon both sides, and submitting it to the satisfactory inspection of every member of the circle, let the medium seat himself at the left of some elderly person, who is spiritually inclined, and allow him to put some bits of pencil upon the upper surface of the slate, afterward placing it under the table-leaf, as shown in figure S., page 149. All the members of the circle should be required to join hands, and, while waiting for the spirits to generate the *périsprit*, a song should be sung, ostensibly for the purpose of harmonizing the circle, *but really to drown any noise emanating from the slate.* During the singing, boldly write with the pencil-thimble a spirit message, in reverse, on the under side of the slate—then, feigning a convulsive movement, withdraw the slate, and, with a flourish, place it upon the table, with the clean side uppermost, saying, "The spirits prefer to write in this open manner." Now place a few bits of pencil under the slate, and diminish the light. Upon the pretext of using your handkerchief, take, by its aid, the pencil-clamp from your pocket and fasten the same to the chine of the table at the point where you are sitting. Then proceed to imitate the sound of writing, with your knee, as shown in figure O, page 203.

This experiment, when properly performed, can hardly fail to be successful, for, the moment the scratching sound of a pencil is heard, the attention of the whole company is invariably concentrated upon the slate, where the writing appears to take place, while, at the conclusion of the noise, they are so deeply engaged in deciphering the message, that all movements on the part of the medium are easily and effectually covered.

Private Sittings. While it is absolutely necessary for every true medium to understand how to properly manage a large spiritual circle, and therein occasionally to practice his art, I would advise those who aspire to eminence as professional mediums not tounderestimate the importance of private sittings.

Many of our best mediums, like Slade, Foster, Watkins, and others, have achieved some of their grandest victories in the presence of a single investigator. There is much less risk of exposure with but one pair of eyes to guard against, than in a circle composed of half-a-dozen, or more, individuals. Five dollars is not a large sum for a wealthy person to pay for the certain assurance of continued life beyond the grave! while five ordinary investigators, who pay one dollar apiece for the same information, even if they fail to audibly grumble at the charge, will, each one of them, inwardly feel that the entire seance should be conducted for his especial benefit. The individual who is willing to pay five dollars for a private sitting is usually a person of some reputation, one who would not be likely to waste his time in an exposure, even though he should detect you in the practice of imposition, while one convert secured from this class is worth more to your professional reputation, and the cause you represent, than the proselytism of a score of ordinary investigators.

Among the various phenomena particularly adapted to the private circle are the spirit-touches in the dark, illustrated by Figures P., Q., and R., page 328.

These very convincing manifestations may be produced in the following manner: Provide yourself with a long feather, and conceal it under your coat, in such a way that the quill-end will be readily accessible to your mouth. Now blindfold your sitter, in order to neutralize the magnetism of his physical eyes, and join hands with him for the space of fifteen or twenty minutes—to the end that the spirits may be enabled to generate the amount of *périsprit* requisite for their grand manifestations—when you can grasp the end of the feather with your teeth, without releasing your hands, and, by its aid, caress the investigator's head and face, until he is convinced, beyond peradventure, that spirits are actually present. Now disengage your hands, and after

Fig. P.

Fig. Q.

Fig. R.

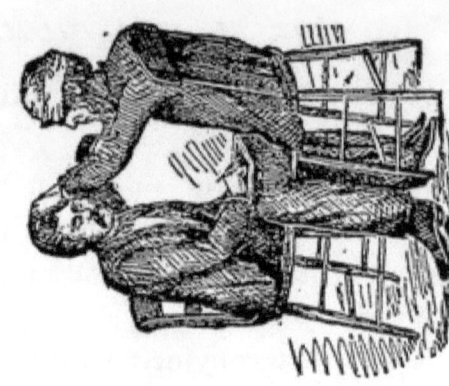

PRIVATE SITTINGS IN THE DARK.

concealing the feather, allow the investigator —still blindfolded—to place both his hands upon your head, with the left upon the right, while you encircle both his arms with your left, grasping his left arm with your left hand. Then lay your right hand lightly upon your left, and press heavily upon his arm with the extended thumb and little finger of the latter, saying, at the same time, "You feel both my hands upon your left arm? Keep close watch of me, that I do not take away either of them!" You will, at once, be able to remove your right hand, and, with it, to assist the spirits to manifest upon the slate, and in many other ways, without the slightest danger of detection on the part of the investigator.

So delusive and absolutely conclusive are these simple experiments, that a large majority of those who participate in a seance of this nature will be fully prepared to affirm, everywhere and always, that the medium, himself, could not possibly have produced the phenomena, for the reason that both his hands were securely held in their own during the entire process of the manifestations!

If you would rank high as a professional medium, be very guarded and reticent in your intercourse with the whole of your professional brethren. Never, in any circumstances, be inveigled into an acknowledgement of any mediumistic powers which they may claim, or the recognition of any spirit-control whatsoever, apart from your own. By strictly adhering to this course, you will command the respecct of the whole fraternity of mediums, many of whom will be inclined to believe that *you* may possibly be genuine, although they know themselves to be frauds.

After you are fairly established in the estimation of the public as a first-class medium, scarcely any mistake, or misdemeanor—save the single vice of drunkenness—will be able to dislodge you from your position. Cultivate sobriety, and keep yourself respectable, and friends who will sustain you in every emergency will swarm to your standard. Like a clairvoyant physician who pretends to interpret character and diagnose physical ailments by the aid of a lock of hair, you will thrive and fatten upon the credulity of the people, and while one clear-headed person may penetrate your deliberate and almost transparent hypocrisy, half a score of new converts will rally to your support.

And, now, having, as I believe, fairly presented, in these pages, the BOTTOM FACTS relating to the science of Spiritualism, I close my labors, commending their results to the calm consideration of those whom I have conscientiously sought to serve.

THE END.

1883. G. W. Carleton & Co. 1883.

NEW BOOKS
AND NEW EDITIONS,
RECENTLY ISSUED BY
G. W. CARLETON & Co., Publishers,
Madison Square, New York.

The Publishers, on receipt of price, send any book on this Catalogue by mail, *postage free*.

All handsomely bound in cloth, with gilt backs suitable for libraries.

Mary J. Holmes' Works.

Tempest and Sunshine	$1 50	Darkness and Daylight	$1 50
English Orphans	1 50	Hugh Worthington	1 50
Homestead on the Hillside	1 50	Cameron Pride	1 50
'Lena Rivers	1 50	Rose Mather	1 50
Meadow Brook	1 50	Ethelyn's Mistake	1 50
Dora Deane	1 50	Millbank	1 50
Cousin Maude	1 50	Edna Browning	1 50
Marian Grey	1 50	West Lawn	1 50
Edith Lyle	1 50	Mildred	1 50
Daisy Thornton	1 50	Forrest House	1 50
Chateau D'Or....(New)	1 50	Madeline......(New)	1 50

Marion Harland's Works.

Alone	$1 50	Sunnybank	$1 50
Hidden Path	1 50	Husbands and Homes	1 50
Moss Side	1 50	Ruby's Husband	1 50
Nemesis	1 50	Phemie's Temptation	1 50
Miriam	1 50	The Empty Heart	1 50
At Last	1 50	Jessamine	1 50
Helen Gardner	1 50	From My Youth Up	1 50
True as Steel....(New)	1 50	My Little Love	1 50

Charles Dickens—15 Vols.—"Carleton's Edition."

Pickwick and Catalogue	$1 50	David Copperfield	$1 50
Dombey and Son	1 50	Nicholas Nickleby	1 50
Bleak House	1 50	Little Dorrit	1 50
Martin Chuzzlewit	1 50	Our Mutual Friend	1 50
Barnaby Rudge—Edwin Drood	1 50	Curiosity Shop—Miscellaneous	1 50
Child's England—Miscellaneous	1 50	Sketches by Boz—Hard Times	1 50
Christmas Books—Two Cities	1 50	Great Expectations—Italy	1 50
		Oliver Twist—Uncommercial	1 50

Sets of Dickens' Complete Works, in 15 vols.—[elegant half calf bindings]... 50 00

Augusta J. Evans' Novels.

Beulah	$1 75	St. Elmo	$2 00
Macaria	1 75	Vashti	2 00
Inez	1 75	Infelice......(New)	2 00

G. W. CARLETON & CO.'S PUBLICATIONS.

May Agnes Fleming's Novels.

Guy Earlscourt's Wife..	$1 50	Heir of Charlton	$1 50
A Wonderful Woman	1 50	Carried by Storm	1 50
A Terrible Secret	1 50	Lost for a Woman	1 50
A Mad Marriage	1 50	A Wife's Tragedy	1 50
Norine's Revenge	1 50	A Changed Heart	1 50
One Night's Mystery	1 50	Pride and Passion	1 50
Kate Danton	1 50	Sharing Her Crime	1 50
Silent and True	1 50	A Wronged Wife.....(New)	1 50

Allan Pinkerton's Works.

Expressmen and Detectives	$1 50	Gypsies and Detectives	$1 50
Mollie Maguires and Detectives	1 50	Spiritualists and Detectives	1 50
Somnambulists and Detectives	1 50	Model Town and Detectives	1 50
Claude Melnotte and Detectives	1 50	Strikers, Communists, etc	1 50
Criminal Reminiscences, etc	1 50	Mississippi Outlaws, etc	1 50
Rail-Road Forger, etc	1 50	Bucholz and Detectives	1 50
Bank Robbers and Detectives	1 50		

Bertha Clay's Novels.

Thrown on the World	$1 50	A Woman's Temptation	$1 50
A Bitter Atonement	1 50	Repented at Leisure	1 50
Love Works Wonders	1 50	Between Two Loves	1 50
Evelyn's Folly	1 50	Lady Damer's Secret	1 50
Under a Shadow....(New)	1 50	A Struggle for a Ring ..(New)	1 50

"New York Weekly" Series.

Brownie's Triumph—Sheldon	$1 50	Curse of Everleigh—Pierce	$1 50
The Forsaken Bride. do.	1 50	Peerless Cathleen—Agnew	1 50
Earle Wayne's Nobility. do.	1 50	Faithful Margaret—Ashmere	1 50
Lost, A Pearle— do. (New)	1 50	Nick Whiffles—Robinson	1 50
A New Book. do.	1 50	Grinder Papers—Dallas	1 50
His Other Wife—Ashleigh	1 50	Lady Leonora—Conklin	1 50

Miriam Coles Harris' Novels.

Rutledge	$1 50	The Sutherlands	$1 50
Frank Warrington	1 50	St. Philips	1 50
Louie's Last Term, St. Mary's	1 50	Round Hearts for Children	1 50
A Perfect Adonis	1 50	Richard Vandermarck	1 50
Missy....(New)	1 50	Happy-Go-Lucky	1 50

A. S. Roe's Select Stories.

True to the Last	$1 50	A Long Look Ahead	$1 50
The Star and the Cloud	1 50	I've Been Thinking	1 50
How Could He Help it?	1 50	To Love and to be Loved	1 50

Julie P. Smith's Novels.

Widow Goldsmith's Daughter	$1 50	The Widower	$1 50
Chris and Otho	1 50	The Married Belle	1 50
Ten Old Maids	1 50	Courting and Farming	1 50
His Young Wife	1 50	Kiss and be Friends	1 50
Lucy	1 50	Blossom Bud.....(New)	1 50

Artemas Ward.

Complete Comic Writings—With Biography, Portrait and 50 illustrations.....$1 50

The Game of Whist.

Pole on Whist—The English standard work. With the "Portland Rules"....$ 75

Victor Hugo's Great Novel.

Les Miserables—Translated from the French. The only complete edition......$1 50

Mrs. Hill's Cook Book.

Mrs. A. P. Hill's New Southern Cookery Book, and domestic receipts.....$2 00

Carleton's Popular Quotations.

Carleton's New Hand-Book—Familiar Quotations, with their authorship ... $1 50
Carleton's Classical Dictionary—Condensed Mythology for popular use...... "5

Celia E. Gardner's Novels.

Stolen Waters. (In verse)	$1 50	Tested	$1 50
Broken Dreams. do.	1 50	Rich Medway	1 50
Compensation. do.	1 50	A Woman's Wiles	1 50
A Twisted Skein. do.	1 50	Terrace Roses	1 50

G. W. CARLETON & CO.'S PUBLICATIONS.

Captain Mayne Reid's Works.
The Scalp Hunters............$1 50 | The White Chief................$1 50
The Rifle Rangers............. 1 50 | The Tiger Hunter............... 1 50
The War Trail................. 1 50 | The Hunter's Feast............. 1 50
The Wood Rangers.............. 1 50 | Wild Life...................... 1 50
The Wild Huntress............. 1 50 | Osceola, the Seminole.......... 1 50

Hand-Books of Society.
The Habits of Good Society—The nice points of taste and good manners.......$1 00
The Art of Conversation—For those who wish to be agreeable talkers......... 1 00
The Arts of Writing, Reading and Speaking—For Self-Improvement............. 1 00
New Diamond Edition—The above 3 books bound in one volume—complete... 1 50

Josh Billings.
His Complete Writings—With Biography, Steel Portrait, and 100 Illustrations.$2 00
Old Probability—Ten Comic Almanax, 1870 to 1879. Bound in one volume..... 1 50

Charles Dickens.
Child's History of England—With *Historical Illustrations* for School use... 75
Parlor Table Album of Dickens' Illustrations—With descriptive text....... 2 50
Lord Bateman Ballad—Notes by Dickens; Pictures by Cruikshank............ 25

Annie Edwardes' Novels.
Stephen Lawrence................$ 75 | Ought We to Visit Her..........$ 75
Susan Fielding.................. 75 | A New Book.................... 75

Ernest Renan's French Works.
The Life of Jesus. Translated....$1 75 | The Life of St. Paul. Translated.$1 75
Lives of the Apostles Do...... 1 75 | The Bible in India—By Jacolliot . 2 00

G. W. Carleton.
Our Artist in Cuba, Peru, Spain, and Algiers—150 Caricatures of travel.......$1 00

M. M. Pomeroy (Brick).
Sense. A serious book...........$1 50 | Nonsense. (A comic book).......$1 50
Gold Dust. Do.............. 1 50 | Brick-dust. Do. 1 50
Our Saturday Nights............. 1 50 | Home Harmonies 1 50

Miscellaneous Works.
Every-Day Home Advice. For Household and Domestic Affairs.............$1 50
The Comic Liar. By the Funny Man of the N. Y. Times. With illustrations.. 1 50
The Children's Fairy Geography—With hundreds of beautiful illustrations... 2 50
Carleton's Popular Readings—Edited by Mrs. Anna Randall Diehl............ 1 50
Laus Veneris, and other Poems—By Algernon Charles Swinburne............. 1 50
Longfellow's Home Life—By Blanche Roosevelt Machetta.................... 1 50
Hawk-eyes—A comic book by "The Burlington Hawkeye Man." Illustrated.. 1 50
Redbirds Christmas Story—An Illustrated Juvenile. By Mary J. Holmes.... 50
The Culprit Fay—Joseph Rodman Drake's Poem. With 100 illustrations..... 2 00
L'Assommoir—English Translation from Zola's famous French novel............ 1 00
Parlor Amusements—Games, Tricks, Home Amusements, by Frank Bellew.... 1 50
Love [L'Amour]—English Translation from Michelet's famous French work... 1 50
Woman [La Femme]—The Sequel to "L'Amour" Do.   Do. 1 50
Verdant Green—A racy English college Story. With 200 comic illustrations... 1 50
Why Wife and I Quarreled—Poem by the Author of "Betsey and I are Out".. 1 00
A Northern Governess at the Sunny South—By Professor J. H. Ingraham.. 1 50
Birds of a Feather Flock Together—By Edward A Sothern, the actor........ 1 50
West India Pickles—A yacht Cruise in the Tropics. By W. P. Talboys....... 1 50
Yachtman's Primer—Instructions for Amateur Sailors. By Warren. 50
The Fall of Man—A Darwinian Satire, by author of "New Gospel of Peace.". 50
The Cronicles of Gotham—A New York Satire. Do.   Do...... 25
Ladies and Gentlemen's Etiquette Book of the best Fashionable Society.... 1 00
Love and Marriage—A book for young people. By Frederick Saunders...... 1 00
Under the Rose—A Capital book, by the author of "East Lynne."............ 1 00
So Dear a Dream—A novel by Miss Grant, author of "The Sun Maid.".......... 1 00
Give me thine Heart—A capital new domestic Love Story by Roe............. 1 00
Meeting Her Fate—A charming novel by the author of "Aurora Floyd."...... 1 00
Faithful to the End—A delightful domestic novel by Roe................... 1 00
Delicate Ground—A powerful new novel by Mrs. Annie Edwardes 1 00

Miscellaneous Works.

Dawn to Noon—By Violet Fane	$1 50
Constance's Fate —Do.	1 50
French Love Songs—Translated	50
A Bad Boy's First Reader	10
Lion Jack—By P. T. Barnum	1 50
Jack in the Jungle—Do.	1 50
Cats, Cooks, Etc—By Edw. T. Ely.	50
Drumming as a Fine Art	50
How to Win in Wall Street	50
The Life of Sarah Bernhardt	25
Arctic Travels—Isaac I. Hayes	1 50
College Tramps—Fred. A. Stokes.	1 50
Gospels in Poetry—E. H. Kimball.	1 50
Me—By Mrs. Spencer W. Coe	50
N. Y. to San Francisco—Leslie	1 50
Don Quixote—Illustrated	$1 00
Arabian Nights—Do.	1 00
Robinson Crusoe Do	1 00
Swiss Family Robinson—Illus.	1 00
Debatable Land—R. Dale Owen	2 00
Threading My Way, Do.	1 50
Spiritualism—By D. D. Home	2 00
Fanny Fern Memorials	2 00
Orpheus C. Kerr—4 vols. in one	2 00
Northern Ballads—E. L. Anderson.	1 00
Offenbach's Tour in America	1 50
Stories about Doctors—Jefferson.	1 50
Stories about Lawyers Do.	1 50
Mrs. Spriggins.—By Widow Bedott	1 50
How to Make Money—Davies	1 50

Miscellaneous Novels.

Doctor Antonio—By Ruffini	$1 50
Beatrice Cenci—From the Italian	1 50
Madame—By Frank Lee Benedict	1 50
A Late Remorse Do.	1 50
Hammer and Anvil Do.	1 50
Her Friend Laurence Do.	1 50
Prairie Flower—Emerson Bennett	1 50
Among the Thorns—Dickinson	1 50
Women of To-day-Mrs. W. H. White	1 50
Braxton's Bar—R. M. Daggett	1 50
Miss Beck—Tilbury Holt	1 50
Sub Rosa—Chas. T. Murray	1 50
Hilda and I—E. Bedell Benjamin	1 50
A College Widow—C. H. Seymour	1 50
Old M'sieur's Secret—Translation.	50
Petticoats and Slippers	50
Shiftless Folks—Fannie Smith	1 50
Peace Pelican. Do.	1 50
Price of a Life—R. Forbes Sturgis.	1 50
Hidden Power—T. H. Tibbles	1 50
Two Brides—Bernard O'Reilly	1 50
Sorry Her Lot—Miss Grant	1 00
Two of Us—Calista Halsey	75
Cupid on Crutches—A. B. Wood	75
Parson Thorne—E. M. Buckingham.	1 50
Marston Hall—L. Ella Byrd	1 50
Ange—Florence Marryatt	1 00
Errors—Ruth Carter	1 50
Unmistakable Flirtation—Garner.	75
Wild Oats—Florence Marryatt	1 50
Widow Cherry—B. L. Farjeon	25
Solomon Isaacs. Do.	50
Edith Murray—Joanna Mathews.	1 50
Doctor Mortimer—Fannie Bean	1 50
Outwitted at Last—S. A. Gardner	1 50
Vesta Vane—L. King. R	1 50
Louise and I—C. R. Dodge	1 50
My Queen—By Sandette	1 50
Fallen among Thieves—Rayne	1 50
San Miniato—Mrs. Hamilton	1 00
All For Her—A Tale of New York	1 50
All for Him—Author "All for Her"	1 50
For Each Other. Do.	1 50
The Baroness—Joaquin Miller	1 50
One Fair Woman. Do.	1 50
Saint Leger—Richard B. Kimball	$1 75
Was He Successful? Do.	1 75
Undercurrents of Wall St. Do.	1 75
Romance of Student Life. Do.	1 75
To-day. Do.	1 75
Life in San Domingo. Do.	1 75
Henry Powers, Banker. Do.	1 75
Led Astray—Octave Feuillet	1 50
She Loved Him Madly—Borys	1 50
Thick and Thin—Mery	1 50
So Fair yet False—Chavette	1 50
A Fatal Passion—C. Bernard	1 50
A Woman's Case—Bessie Turner.	1 50
Marguerite's Journal—For Girls.	1 50
Rose of Memphis—W. C. Falkner.	1 50
Spell-Bound—Alexandre Dumas	75
Heart's Delight—Mrs. Alderdice.	1 50
Another Man's Wife—Mrs. Hartt.	1 50
Purple and Fine Linen—Fawcett.	1 50
Pauline's Trial—L. D. Courtney.	1 50
The Forgiving Kiss—M. Loth	1 75
Flirtation—A West Point novel.	1 50
Loyal unto Death	1 50
That Awful Boy	50
That Bridget of Ours	50
Phemie Frost—Ann S. Stephens	1 50
Charette—An American novel	1 50
Fairfax—Jo. n Esten Cooke	1 50
Hilt to Hilt. Do.	1 50
Out of the Foam. Do.	1 50
Hammer and Rapier. Do.	1 50
Warwick—By M. T. Walworth	1 75
Lulu. Do.	1 75
Hotspur Do.	1 75
Stormcliff. Do.	1 75
Delaplaine. Do.	1 75
Beverly. Do.	1 75
Kenneth—Sallie A. Brock	1 75
Heart Hungry—Westmoreland	1 50
Clifford Troupe. Do.	1 50
Silcott Mill—Maria D. Deslonde	1 50
John Maribel. Do.	1 50
Conquered—By a New Author	1 50
Janet—An English novel	1 50
Tales from the Popular Operas	1 50

www.ingramcontent.com/pod-product-compliance
Lightning Source LLC
Chambersburg PA
CBHW030302240426
43673CB00040B/1030